C. GENE WILKES

JESUS
ON LEADERSHIP

Becoming A Servant Leader

STUDENT EDITION

LIFEWAY PRESS
NASHVILLE, TENNESSEE

This workbook is the resource for course CG-0514 in the
subject area Ministry of the
Christian Growth Study Plan.

Dewey Decimal Classification: 303.3
Subject Heading: Leadership

Unless otherwise indicated, Scripture quotations are from
the Holy Bible, *New International Version*, copyright ©
1973, 1978, 1984 by International Bible Society.
Used by permission.

A Spanish edition for adults also is available, ISBN 0-7673-
2668-7

Printed in the United States of America
Available from Customer Service Center,
1-800-458-BSSB and LifeWay Christian Stores/Baptist Book
Stores

Youth Section
Discipleship and Family Group
LifeWay Christian Resources
of the Southern Baptist Convention
127 Ninth Avenue North
Nashville, Tennessee 37234-0152

TABLE OF CONTENTS

For even the Son of Man did not come to be served, but to serve, and to give his life as a ransom for many (Mark 10:45).

Each one should use whatever gift he has received to serve others, faithfully administering God's grace in its various forms (1 Pet. 4:10).

But he said to me, "My grace is sufficient for you, for my power is made perfect in weakness." Therefore I will boast all the more gladly about my weaknesses, so that Christ's power may rest on me (2 Cor. 12:9).

It was he who gave some to be apostles, some to be prophets, some to be evangelists, and some to be pastors and teachers, to prepare God's people for works of service, so that the body of Christ may be built up (Eph. 4:11-12).

Calling the Twelve to him, he sent them out two by two and gave them authority over evil spirits (Mark 6:7).

INTRODUCTION

If you are reading this sentence, you may be a leader. Someone has handed you this workbook because he or she thinks you have the potential to become a leader in your youth group or church. You may be thinking they were wrong in their choice, but you have the potential of being a leader if you will follow the examples and teachings of Jesus on leadership.

You may think leadership among youth is confined to student body presidents or people chosen as athletic, music or organization leaders. You may also believe that if you are not a leader at school, there's no way you can lead at church. Leadership among God's people, however, is not limited to those whom the world elects or appoints as leaders. You can be a servant leader just like Jesus if you will pay close attention to the teachings in this workbook.

Jesus On Leadership, Student Edition, has been edited with you in mind. Stacey Whitt, youth minister at Legacy Drive Baptist Church, Plano, TX, and Gene Wilkes, writer of the adult version of Jesus on Leadership and pastor at Legacy Drive, have edited this workbook to help you become a servant leader like Jesus. We have chosen stories of people just like you who are learning to lead like Jesus. We have tried in every way to make Jesus' teachings and examples of being a leader as clear as possible so you can apply them to your life at church, school, and home. We know the church needs leaders from your generation now more than ever. We are praying that God will show you where and how you are to serve as a leader in your youth group and church.

You are at a strategic time in your life. You are preparing to live as a responsible, godly adult. Every choice you make now will affect how you live as an adult. Our hope is that you take these next six weeks to learn to lead like Jesus. We want you to know how God is forming you into a unique servant leader will affect your life in a positive way.

As you begin, turn to page 127 in this workbook. There you see the four concepts you need to know in order to see the overview of this study. Those four concepts are servant leader, serve, equip and team. In week 1, you will learn seven principles of servant leadership from the life and teachings of Jesus. We will spend weeks 2 and 3 discovering how God made you as a unique servant leader by developing your own S.E.R.V.E. Profile. Weeks 4 and 5 answer the question, "What do servant leaders do?" The answer is, "They equip others for ministry and build a ministry team."

Now that you know where we are headed, let's go!

THIS WEEK'S
MEMORY VERSE

"For even the Son of Man did not come to be served, but to serve, and to give his life as a ransom for many" (Mark 10:45, NIV).

When I was in high school, I ran for student body president. I ended up running against a good friend and another guy I thought would never have a chance to win. I made posters and asked people to vote for me. After the votes were counted, the guy I thought had no chance to win was elected president! I was devastated. I began to wonder if I would ever be a leader if I could not even win an election that made you a leader. *How could you lead, if people didn't elect you to lead, I wondered. How can you be a leader if you are never asked to sit at a head table and make a speech,* I also thought. I waited for another chance to be elected or appointed a leader.

Later in college, I decided to run for president of the service organization I had joined. Again, I ended up running against a good friend, and, yes, again, I was not elected president. This time my friend won, and I was elected sergeant at arms. I wondered if I would ever be a leader. I still thought you had to be elected to an office or sit at the head table at some awards banquet to be a leader. So, I waited for God to make me a leader.

Without boring you with all the details, I will tell you I have never been elected to any position of leadership and have sat at very few head tables. But, I am a leader. I am the pastor of a growing church that helps people know, share, and multiply Christ in the lives of others. I am a husband and father. Each of these rolls is a position of leadership. Each of these places gives me an opportunity to lead others.

Why do I tell you these facts about my life? I tell them to you because you may be thinking like I thought. If you don't get elected or invited to sit at a head table, you must not be a leader. Jesus, on the other hand, teaches us something different about being a leader among God's people. Jesus taught that service, not status is the goal of a leader who has Christ as his master.

Many churches and youth ministries struggle because they lack servant leaders. In too many churches today, head tables have replaced the towel and washbasin as symbols of leadership among God's people. Often those recognized as leaders hold positions elected by their friends and family. Some of these leaders love sitting at head tables and never go near the kitchen or nursery. Churches and youth groups need leaders who know how God has gifted them for service and who are willing to serve Christ's body. Churches and youth ministries need leaders who know their mission and can equip others to help them carry out that mission.

Churches and youth ministries need leaders who will step down from the head table and serve wherever they are needed. Churches in the 21st century need teenagers and college students who will stop following the world's concepts of leadership and adopt Jesus' teachings and examples of servant leadership.

Servant leadership is not an oxymoron![1] Servant and leader do stand together as a model for persons entrusted with the well-being of a group.

> Many churches struggle because they lack servant leaders.
> In too many churches today, head tables have replaced the towel and washbasin as symbols of leadership among God's people.

Leadership through service is how Jesus modeled and taught discipleship among His closest friends. True servant leadership begins by submitting to Jesus and obediently following His teachings and lifestyle as a leader. You can lead like Jesus only when you obey His teachings about leading as a servant.

When we observe Jesus' life, we see He was first servant to the Father's mission for His life. That mission was to be the Suffering Servant Messiah *(Isa. 53:11)*, to lay down *his life as a ransom for many (Mark 10:45)*. Jesus humbled Himself and became a servant to God's mission for His life *(Phil. 2:6-8)*. We also see that Jesus led by serving those He recruited to carry out the Father's mission after He ascended to heaven. Jesus was a leader, but the focus of His leadership was empowering others to live out God's plan, not their own agendas. He served His disciples with the vision, direction, correction, and resources needed to complete the mission the Father sent Him to do. Jesus was a servant to the Father's mission, and He led by serving those on mission with Him. Jesus was a servant leader. These observations about Jesus' life are the basis for our working definition of a servant leader:

> **A servant leader serves the mission and leads by serving those on mission with Him.**[2]

The purpose of this study is to help your church and student ministry add a service dimension to leadership as you discover, equip, and place servant leaders in all areas of your ministry. Jesus' teachings and modeling of servant leadership are the foundation for this study. Also, this study can lead members of the body of Christ to discover their role as servant leaders, and to equip them for team ministry. Servant leaders in team ministry, that is our purpose together as individual members and as a church.

My prayer is that churches will begin to honor and train leaders who willingly follow Jesus' teachings and model of servant leadership. My personal goal is to serve you and your church through this workbook and to help restore a biblical model of servant leadership in your church.

This Week You Will:
- Discover seven principles of servant leadership. (Days 1-4)
- Examine definitions of servant leadership and Jesus' teachings about humility. (Day 1)
- Examine Jesus' teachings about being first and being great. (Day 2)
- Observe Jesus' model of servant leadership through His actions on the night He was betrayed. (Day 3)
- Examine biblical models of shared leadership. (Day 4)
- Evaluate God's calling in your life to be a servant leader. (Day 5)

> Servant leaders in team ministry, that is our purpose together as individual members and as a church.

day 1

JESUS' TEACHINGS ON LEADERSHIP–PART 1

"Leadership is more than one person in a visible leadership role. It also involves service in quieter, less noticeable ways."[3] —Wes Black

Today You Will:
- Review the biblical concept of servant leadership.
- Examine Jesus' teachings about humility.
- Take inventory of your relationship with Jesus Christ.
- Study Jesus' model of humble service to all.

Today, we want to examine different ideas about leadership. We want to spend our time with biblical models of leadership and how Jesus taught and modeled leadership for His followers. Let's start with your impressions of a leader. Below you will find a list of character traits. Place a check beside those qualities you consider important in a leader.

❏ Honest	❏ Kind	❏ Fair	❏ Goal-oriented
❏ Humble	❏ Bold	❏ Caring	❏ Has Integrity
❏ Godly	❏ Above Average	❏ Serving	❏ Is Inspiring
❏ Dependable	❏ Emotional	❏ Decisive	❏ Cautious
❏ Cooperative	❏ Independent	❏ Loyal	❏ Intelligent

Return to the list and circle those characteristics that are present in your own life.

People know what they want in a leader. Some prefer that the leader be decisive or visionary. Others want their leader to be charming and kind to people. Some desire not to have a leader, thank you very much!

I want to highlight the trait of service. A leader with a heart for service serves the mission of God on his life and leads by serving those he leads in order for the group to complete its mission. This kind of leader leads by example and service rather than by telling people what to do.

Leadership in the kingdom of God is different from leadership in the world. It is still leadership, but those who lead in the kingdom of God look very different from those who lead by the world's standards. Life under the lordship of Christ has different values than life under the lordship of self. Therefore, kingdom leaders are people who lead like Jesus. They act differently than leaders trained by the world. Kingdom leaders are servant leaders because they follow Jesus, who *"did not come to be served, but to serve"* (Mark 10:45).

People prefer to follow those who help them, not those who intimidate them!

An attitude that keeps you from leading like Jesus is what we call "head table mentality." It is simply the attitude that you feel if you are seated at the head table then you must be more important than others. Head table mentality is also the belief that your goal is to sit at the head table. Important people and leaders sit up front. The ordinary people sit out with the others. The thought of sitting out with everyone else is not where you want to be! These attitudes prevent you from being a leader like Jesus. Here's why.

Jesus taught His disciples a valuable lesson about head tables and a humble spirit.

Jesus' ideas about leadership are different from the world's thoughts on leadership.

Jesus' Story About Humility

Read *Luke 14:1,7-11.* Then think about the following questions:

1. Where was Jesus when He told this story? *(Luke 14:1)*

2. Why did He tell the story? *(Luke 14:7)*

3. Put yourself in the disciples' sandals. What would be your response to Jesus' message in that place to those people?

Jesus told this story to His followers while they attended a meal at the house of a prominent religious leader. He noticed how the guests picked places of honor at the head table near the host. He chose this situation to teach His disciples how they should behave toward places of honor. Write the main point of each of the verses in the parable:

Verse 8:

Verse 9:

Verse 10:

Verse 11:

Jesus said that those who follow Him must first humble themselves. Any head-table recognition should come from others. Final recognition will come from God. The world says, "Work your way to the head table." Jesus says, "Take a seat in the back. I'll choose who sits up front."

The word *humble* in *verse 11* means to "make low or humiliate by assigning to a low(er) place."[4] Jesus called His disciples to lower themselves rather than exalt themselves. He made it clear that His followers were not to seek places of honor. Jesus' disciples wait for their Host to invite them to the head table. They do not seek high places on their own. The Bible says, *humility comes before honor (Prov. 15:33).*

The first principle of servant leadership is: Servant leaders humble themselves and wait for God to exalt them.

You cannot apply this first principle of a servant leader to your own life unless you commit yourself to follow Jesus' teachings. You must decide whether or not you will design your life after the pattern of Jesus, or design your life around the best thinking and experience the world has to offer.

Decision Point: Before we go any further, you must settle this issue in your life. You must answer the question, "Who is Master of my life?" Here's why your answer to that question is basic to this study:

No one can be a servant without a master. You cannot be a servant leader as modeled by Jesus without Him as your Master. Jesus said you can't serve two masters. You will either hate the one and love the other, or you will be devoted to one and despise the other. *(See Matt. 6:24.)* Leaders without Jesus as their Master can only be self-serving, not serving to others.

Take a moment to examine your heart and answer the following questions:

1. Have I confessed my sinfulness and resistance to God's leadership in my life? ❏ Yes ❏ No

2. Have I confessed that Jesus is Lord of my life? *(See Rom. 10:9.)*
   ❏ Yes ❏ No

3. Do I live my life as if I am in control or as if Christ is in control? *(See Gal. 2:20.)* ❏ I am ❏ Christ is

4. Have I shown a willingness to humble myself before others, or am I happier when I earn a seat at a head table?
   ❏ I humble myself. ❏ I love earning my seat.

The answers to these questions help describe your relationship with Jesus Christ. The rest of this workbook will only be exercises in self will if Christ is not in control of every aspect of your life. If you want to settle this issue in your life right now, pause and ask Christ to be Lord and Savior of your life. Then, call your group's leader or your youth minister and ask this person to join you in prayer. Be prepared to share your decision at the next group meeting.

An Attitude Like Jesus

The apostle Paul asked the Christians in Philippi to serve each other like Jesus would serve them. Paul reminded his friends of their source of strength, fellowship, and unity in Christ. He wrote, *"Your attitude should be the same as that of Christ Jesus" (Phil. 2:5).* Paul then described Jesus' humble service of taking on the form of a man and dying on the cross for others.

> *You must decide whether or not you will design your life after the pattern of Jesus, or design your life around the best thinking and experience the world has to offer.*

Read *Philippians 2:6-11*, which is printed below. Underline the words that describe how Jesus humbled Himself. Then go through the verses again and circle the words that tell how God exalted Him.

> "Your attitude should
> be the same as that
> of Christ Jesus"
> (Phil. 2:5).

> Who, being in very nature God,
> did not consider equality with God
> something to be grasped,
> but made himself nothing,
> taking the very nature of a servant,
> being made in human likeness.
> And being found in appearance as a man,
> he humbled himself
> and became obedient to death—
> even death on a cross!
> Therefore God exalted him to the highest place
> and gave him the name that is above every name,
> that at the name of Jesus every knee should bow,
> in heaven and on earth and under the earth,
> and every tongue confess that Jesus Christ is Lord,
> to the glory of God the Father.

The key phrase in the first half of this passage is, *he humbled himself (Phil. 2:8)*. Paul's term for *humble* is the same word Jesus used in His story to the disciples in *Luke 14:7-11*. Jesus taught humility because it was at the core of who He was. It was God's plan for His Son's life. The key phrase in the second half of these verses is, *God exalted him (v. 11)*. Paul's word for *exalt* is also the same word Jesus used in His story in Luke. God exalted His Son after Jesus humbled Himself in obedience to death on the cross. Peter, who was present as Jesus taught this lesson about humility recorded in *Luke 14*, told the early Christians to *Humble yourselves, therefore, under God's mighty hand, that he may lift you up in due time (1 Pet. 5:6)*.

Servant leaders among God's people humble themselves in obedience to Christ. Exaltation is God's choice, not ours. Leaders like Jesus must have the humble spirit of Christ and must be willing to take the seats in the back. God will choose those who will be up front.

Personal Review

Prayerfully take time to consider your answers to the following questions.

- Am I trusted as a leader because people see me as a servant?
  - ❑ Yes ❑ No
- Am I willing to wait on the invitation of the Host to sit at the head table? ❑ Yes ❑ No
- Do people see the humility of Christ in my life?
  - ❑ Yes ❑ No

- Is Jesus genuinely Master of my life?
  - ❐ Yes ❐ No
- Am I willing to humble myself like Jesus in order to allow God to accomplish His plan for my life?
  - ❐ Yes ❐ No

Principles of Servant Leadership:

Principle 1: Servant leaders _____ themselves and wait for God to _____ them.

Summary

- The first principle of servant leadership is: Servant leaders humble themselves and wait for God to exalt them.
- True leadership begins with a servant's heart.
- Jesus taught His disciples not to seek places at the head table.
- Jesus must be your Master before you can be a servant leader like Him.
- Jesus modeled a servant's heart in His incarnation and His crucifixion.

[1]An oxymoron is a figure of speech in which opposite or contradictory ideas or terms are combined. A favorite example is *civil war* or *bitter sweet*.

[2]C. Gene Wilkes, *Jesus on Leadership: Discovering the Secrets of Servant Leadership from the Life of Christ* (Carol Stream, IL: Tyndale, 1998), 18.

[3]*An Introduction to Youth Ministry,* (Broadman Press, 1991), 123.

[4]William F. Arndt and Wilbur F. Gingrich, *A Greek-English Lexicon of the New Testament and Other Early Christian Literature* (Chicago: University of Chicago Press, 1957), 812.

Again, here is this week's memory verse, this time with a few of the words omitted. Complete the verse. As you complete today's work, read these words of Jesus aloud a few times. Spend a few more moments alone with God, and listen to Him speak to your heart concerning servant leadership.

"For even the _____ did not come to be _____, but to serve, and to ___ his life as a _____ for many" (Mark 10:45, NIV).

day 2

JESUS' TEACHINGS ON LEADERSHIP-PART 2

The number one quality that must mark tomorrow's leaders is servanthood.[1]

—Calvin Miller

Today You Will:

- Observe James' and John's request of Jesus.
- Define greatness and being first as taught by Jesus.
- Discover the second and third principles of servant leadership.
- Reflect on the biblical event recorded in *Mark 10* and write ways you can be great and first.

Every Wednesday night over 500 feet of speaker cables, 300 pounds of sound equipment, a video projector and screen along with 80 to 90 chairs are put into place before a herd of teenagers invade what we affectionately call "The Barn" for our mid-week youth worship service. Our set-up time usually begins at 4:00 p.m. every Wednesday afternoon, and just like clock work in walks Justin. Quietly he throws off his backpack and starts setting up all the stuff that makes our youth worship service happen. Justin never seeks to be up front unless duty calls. Most of the time he's either helping out with the youth tech team or hanging out at the back of "The Barn" waiting for another chance to serve. Many of the youth who are there each Wednesday night are not even aware that their chair and sound equipment was put in place by a peer who lives the life of a servant. Justin is a servant leader.

You may have a Justin (or a girl like him) in your youth group. This person's first move is to serve others. This kind of leadership flows out of his service to God's mission and to others.

Jesus re-defined greatness and being first when He declared: *"Whoever wants to become great among you must be your servant, and whoever wants to be first must be slave of all" (Mark 10:43-44).* You are great when you serve. You are first when you are a slave. Jesus taught this to His closest disciples. These men had accepted Jesus' call to follow Him. They would lead others in the work of God after Jesus ascended to the right hand of the Father. How they understood leadership among God's people was crucial to how kingdom people would live together in generations to come.

Jesus taught about greatness and being first after James and John had asked Him a favor. Take a look at what happened to cause Jesus to teach His disciples about servant leadership.

> You are great when you serve. You are first when you are a slave. Jesus taught this to His closest disciples.

James, John, and You

Read *Mark 10:32-40*. Answer the following questions after you have read the passage.

1. What did James and John ask Jesus? *(Mark 10:37)*

2. What had Jesus said that caused them to ask the question? *(Mark 10:33-34)*

3. What was Jesus' reply to their question? *(Mark 10:38)*

4. How did James and John reply to Jesus' comments? *(Mark 10:39)*

5. Finally, what did Jesus say to them? *(Mark 10:39-40)*

6. What do you think of James' and John's request? Write your opinion below:

James and John sensed that something important would happen in Jerusalem. They thought Jesus was getting close to His throne, and selfishly they wanted to lead from positions of power beside Him. James and John thought kingdom leadership meant a position or title. They betrayed their ambitious hearts by getting to Jesus first.

Before you judge these two brothers, remember that we are very much like them. We, too, want places up front when Jesus defeats His enemies. We forget, however, that *suffering like Jesus comes before reigning with Jesus*. Jesus wanted James and John to know that following Him would cost them their lives, not gain them places at the head table. Only the Host knows who sits there.

The second principle of servant leadership is: Servant leaders follow Jesus rather than seek a position.

Calvin Miller has noted that servant leadership "is nurtured in the Spirit by following Jesus. Servant leaders generally are created not in commanding others but in obeying their Commander."[2] Don't get confused by thinking that if you have a position of leadership you don't have to follow anyone. Servant leaders follow Jesus before they lead others.

Servant leadership is not about position and power. Leaders among Christ's disciples follow Jesus as He serves others and suffers on their behalf. Servant leadership requires drinking the cup and being baptized with the baptism of Christ's suffering *(Mark 10:38-39)*.

> *Jesus wanted James and John to know that following Him would cost them their lives, not gain them places at the head table.*

The Other 10 Disciples and You

Read *Mark 10:41-45*. Put yourself in the other 10 disciples' sandals when they heard about James' and John's request, and answer the following questions.

1. Were the other disciples' feelings toward James and John justified? *(Mark 10:41)* ❏ Yes ❏ No   Why or why not?

2. When Jesus called the group together, how did He describe the world's concept of leadership? *(Mark 10:42)*

3. Write your own definition of "lord it over."

4. Write your own definition of "exercise authority."

5. Jesus said that the way the world practices leadership would not be the pattern among His true disciples. Fill in the blanks with the words of Jesus from *Mark 10:43*:
   "*Whoever wants to become _____ among you must be your _____, and whoever wants to be _____ must be _____ of all.*"

6. We get our English prefix *mega* from the Greek word for great. Our English word *deacon* comes from the Greek word for servant. This *servant* in the ancient world waited on tables. Write your understanding of Christlike greatness based on this information.

7. We get our English prefix *proto* from the Greek word for first. It means first in a series or line. No single English word adequately describes the Greek word for *slave (doulos)* in this passage. Such a *slave* was on the lowest rung of the social ladder. The owner bought and sold slaves like household goods. The *doulos* was a bond-slave who served the master without will or question. A slave had no rights or privileges, no wants or desires, only the commands of the master. Write your understanding of being first among the disciples of Jesus based upon this information.

The third principle of servant leadership is: Servant leaders give up personal rights to find greatness in service to others.

Jesus said that the way the world practices leadership would not be the pattern among His true disciples.

Jesus re-defined greatness and being first. When you make Jesus Master in your life, you become a servant to others. To lead in the Kingdom of God is to serve others and to follow the King.

Jesus, The Servant Leader

Jesus defined greatness as the life of a servant. What does this picture of leadership look like in real life today? How can servants and slaves really lead? The answer poses a real dilemma for a disciple of Jesus.

You won't find servants and slaves under *leadership* in the world's dictionary. Many persons understand the idea of being a servant and forfeiting personal rights as portraying a negative self-image. Jesus came to show what life in the kingdom of God looks like, not to modify how the world does things. The ways of God only work in the hallways at school when Jesus reigns in students hearts. Any follower of Christ who seeks to lead like Jesus must be willing to be treated like Jesus.

Some will follow. Others will throw stones.

By example, Jesus answered the question of how to lead like a servant. He concluded, *"For even the Son of Man did not come to be served, but to serve, and to give his life as a ransom for many" (Mark 10:45).* Jesus was not a teacher who only defined His terms. He also modeled what He called others to do. James, John, and the other 10 disciples experienced what Jesus taught as they followed Him to His death. They soon learned that servant leadership ultimately means giving up your self so that others can have the life God desires for them.

Jesus deserves service from those He created! He, however, came to serve us. Jesus came to give His life as a ransom so that we could be set free from sin. A ransom in the ancient world was a payment to free a slave or prisoner.[3] As the Son of Man, Jesus saw His life as one of sacrifice so that others could be freed.

Jesus is our only true model of servant leadership. He served others by giving His life for them. His entire mission was to free others, not to gain position for Himself. This is a mystery to the world, but it is the heart of kingdom leadership. Anyone who seeks to lead in the body of Christ must submit himself or herself to the lordship of Jesus. Only then can one begin to understand why servants are great and slaves are first.

Personal Evaluation

Jesus responded to the wishes of His disciples and taught them about servant leadership. Consider your responses to the following statements. Prayerfully write your feelings and thoughts.

I am like James and John because I . . .

> Any follower of Christ who seeks to lead like Jesus must be willing to be treated like Jesus. Some will follow. Others will throw stones.

I am like the other 10 disciples because I . . .

I can be "great" as a servant this week by . . .

I can be "first" as a slave this week by . . .

Principles of Servant Leadership

Principle 1: Servant leaders _____ themselves and wait for God to _____ them.

Principle 2: Servant leaders _____ Jesus rather than seek a _____.

Principle 3: Servant leaders give up personal _____ to find greatness in _____ to others.

Summary

• The second principle of servant leadership is: Servant leaders follow Jesus rather than seek a position.

• The third principle of servant leadership is: Servant leaders give up personal rights to find greatness in service to others.

• Jesus re-defined greatness and being first when He declared: *"Whoever wants to become great among you must be your servant, and whoever wants to be first must be slave of all"* (Mark 10:43-44).

• James and John thought kingdom leadership meant a position or title.

• Jesus deserves service from all those He created! He, however, came not to be served, but to serve. He came to give His life as a ransom to free others.

[1] Calvin Miller, *The Empowered Leader: 10 Keys to Servant Leadership* (Nashville: Broadman & Holman, 1995), 17.

[2] Ibid., 18.

[3] Arndt and Gingrich, 483.

Again, here is this week's memory verse. As you complete today's work, read these words again, and then take a few moments to listen as God speaks.

"For even the Son of Man did not come to be served, but to serve, and to give his life as a ransom for many" (Mark 10:45).

Now try covering the verse and writing it from memory in the space here. Don't worry if you can't yet write it word for word. By the end of the week, God will plant the words firmly in your heart, and its meaning will grow.

day 3

JESUS' MODEL OF LEADERSHIP

Christian leaders should adopt the leadership style of Jesus, who washed His disciples' feet. Interestingly, the "old style" of Jesus is as up-to-date as modern leadership theory.[1]

—*Leith Anderson*

Today You Will:
- Discover the fourth and fifth principles of servant leadership.
- Discover the power of servant leadership by examining John's statements about Jesus before He washed His disciples' feet.
- Observe how Jesus left His place at the table and washed His disciples' feet.
- Evaluate your feelings as a leader about washing the feet of others.
- Test your knowledge of Jesus' model of servant leadership.

The Power of Servant Leadership

Some people love to take risks. My oldest daughter came home one day from a trip to a local theme park and told us she had ridden one of those 90-foot swings. Her mother was angry she took such a risk, I wanted to know if you really go 70 mph after they drop you. Some people take risks easily. Others are more cautious. Being a leader like Jesus means taking risks. It means being willing to get up from your place of leadership to help others complete the mission God gave you to do. You must be willing to risk your position of leadership so others can succeed.

John 13 tells the story of Jesus' last meal with His disciples. At that meal, Jesus modeled for all time what servant leadership looks like by washing His disciples' feet. John, under the inspiration of the Holy Spirit, noted some things about Jesus before He took up the towel and basin. *These facts reveal the secret to risking servant leadership.*

Read *John 13:3*. List the statements that describe what Jesus knew about Himself at this time.

1.

2.

3.

> *Jesus modeled for all time what servant leadership looks like.*

Jesus knew that God had "put all things under his power." He knew that God was in control of His life and ministry. He knew His place as the Son of God. Jesus knew "He had come from God." He knew that God was the source of His mission on earth. He was confident that what He was doing was part of God's ultimate plan for His life. Jesus knew He "was returning to God." He knew that He would return to His eternal place as God in heaven. Jesus' knowledge of these facts, John wrote, preceded His act to take up the towel and basin. Confident of these facts, Jesus was able to model what God had sent Him to do: to serve others and to give His life.

Circle the number that represents your trust in God in these areas of your life (1 being most like you, and 5 being least like you).

1. I trust that in Christ God has given me power to serve others.

1 2 3 4 5   (See *Eph.* 2:6-7 for your place "in Christ.")

2. I trust that God created me and has a plan for my life.

1 2 3 4 5

3. I trust that I will go to be with God at my death.

1 2 3 4 5

These facts of faith are the source of power that allow you to risk leading others as a servant. You are secure enough to brave serving others only when your security is in God and not self. Without God-centered certainty, you have no choice but to protect ego and defend your rights. Only when you trust God with absolute control of your life can you risk losing your self in service to others.

> **The fourth principle of servant leadership is: Servant leaders can risk serving others because they trust that God is in control of their lives.**

Jesus knew His power was from God. He knew He came from and was returning to God. The secret to risking servant leadership is the assurance that God is in control of your life.

The Ministry of The Towel

I have a towel in my office with shoe polish on it. I only use it when the church sets apart members of our church as deacons. Each time they do this, I get on my knees and wipe the dust from their shoes in front of the entire church. I do this for two reasons: (1) to remind myself of my role as their servant leader; and (2) I want each of them to remember Jesus' example of servant leadership when He washed His disciples' feet.

Jesus performed two symbolic acts for His followers on the night He was betrayed. He took up a servant's towel and washbasin and washed their feet. He also took the bread and wine from the Passover meal and announced a new covenant between God and His creation in the blood of Jesus.

The secret to risking servant leadership is the assurance that God is in control of your life.

When Jesus asked His disciples to prepare the Passover meal, He did not tell them to hire a servant. Jesus wanted His closest followers to learn an important lesson that night.

Read *John 13:4-11*. In your own words, describe what Jesus did.

1. When Jesus came to Peter, the "fisher of men" resisted Jesus. Why do you think Peter said what he did *(John 13:6,8)*? How do you relate to what he said?

2. How did Jesus respond to Peter's resistance? What did He say *(John 13:7-8)*?

Jesus surprised His followers when He left the head table and moved to where servants worked. He took off His outer clothes and picked up a servant's towel. He wrapped the towel around His waist, filled a basin with water, and began to wash the dusty feet of His friends. This was not His job. He was Teacher and Lord. Yet Jesus re-defined what leaders do: *leaders meet needs* to make sure everyone knows the mission. Jesus' followers had dirty feet, and no one was willing to wash them. They had a need, but no one would leave his place to meet it.

Jesus modeled servant leadership when He willingly left His place at the table and knelt down to meet needs of His followers—needs that were both physical and spiritual. Peter's response to Jesus' actions revealed that he did not understand at first. Nobody does. Jesus could only say, "You will understand later." Jesus' descent from the Passover meal to the servant's towel and washbasin parallels His descent from heaven to the cross *(Phil. 2:5-11)*. His actions also modeled what He had taught earlier about being great and first *(Mark 10:35-45)*. The Teacher modeled in the upper room what He had taught earlier on the road to Jerusalem.

> **The fifth principle of servant leadership is: Servant leaders take up Jesus' towel of servanthood to meet the needs of others.**

Important Note: Meeting needs does not necessarily mean giving in to people's wishes. Jesus knelt as a servant at Peter's feet, but He did not allow Peter's personal preference to keep Him from His mission. Peter did not get his way. Servanthood does not mean just doing what someone selfishly wants. Servants cannot waver from doing their master's wishes.

Leaders sometimes must reveal a need before meeting it. Your parents bathed you as a child even though you did not feel being clean was important!

Another Important Note: Jesus also washed the feet of Judas, the disciple who would betray Him with a kiss. Knowing that Judas would turn Him

Your greatest test of servant leadership may be to wash the feet of those you know will soon betray you.

over to the religious leaders to be crucified, Jesus still washed his feet. Your greatest test of servant leadership may be to wash the feet of those you know will soon betray you.

Jesus modeled for all what kingdom leadership looks like. Seeking to lead like Jesus means you must be willing to give up your position in order to serve, and kneel at the dirty feet of others. Sometimes that means revealing a need in order to meet it. At other times, it means humbling yourself before the very ones who will turn you over to your enemies.

An Example For All to Follow

Read *John 13:12-17.* When Jesus finished washing the disciples' feet, He put on His outer clothes and returned to His place at the table. He had acted out His lesson. And He wanted to know if His students understood *(John 13:12).* Jesus agreed with His followers that He was their Teacher and Lord.

1. What did He say after that *(John 13:14)?*

Jesus said that He was His disciples' teacher and master. Since that was true, He said, they must do what He commanded them to do. He said they should *"wash one another's feet"* *(John 13:14).*

2. Write some ways you could "wash the feet" of those you know.

Jesus said that He set an example for His disciples to follow *(John 13:15).* The word *example* means "to show under the eyes as an illustration or warning." Jesus modeled behavior He wanted His followers to imitate.

3. How did Jesus conclude His lesson in servant leadership? What truth did He state *(John 13:16)?*

Jesus said, *"As my servants and those whom I have sent, you are to do what I have done."* Those who lead in the kingdom of God must check where they sit and what they wear. If you are not wearing a servant's towel kneeling at the feet of others, you are in the wrong place.

Those who lead in God's kingdom lead from a kneeling position, dressed like a servant, acting like a slave to meet the needs of those who follow them so all can complete God's mission.

4. Jesus made a promise to His disciples at the end of His lesson. What was it *(John 13:17)?*

Jesus said that you will receive a blessing when you serve others like He did. God blesses those who take up the towel and washbasin like His Son.

Personal Evaluation

Thinking about what you have learned from today's study, place a T (true) or F (false) beside the statements below.

___ 1. You can be a servant leader by deciding in your own power to act like Jesus.

> *If you are not wearing a servant's towel kneeling at the feet of others, you are in the wrong place.*

___ 2. You can risk being a servant leader when you trust that God is in control of your life.

___ 3. The symbols of Christlike leadership are a towel and a washbasin.

___ 4. Servant leaders lead from a kneeling position.

___ 5. Jesus should have honored Peter's request not to wash his feet.

___ 6. If Jesus led with the towel, so should His followers.

___ 7. You will be blessed if you do as Jesus did.

___ 8. You can serve others when you trust that God is in control of your life and that God is your beginning and your end.

___ 9. A leader models servant leadership when he leaves his position at the head table, takes up tools of service, and kneels at the feet of others to meet a need.

___ 10. Jesus modeled what He had taught about being great and first by His actions on the night He was betrayed *(Mark 10:35-45)*.

Principles of Servant Leadership

Principle 1: Servant leaders _____ themselves and wait for God to _____ them.

Principle 2: Servant leaders _____ Jesus rather than seek a _____.

Principle 3: Servant leaders give up personal _____ to find greatness in _____ to others.

Principle 4: Servant leaders can risk serving others because they _____ that God is in _____ of their lives.

Principle 5: Servant leaders take up Jesus' towel of _____ to meet the needs of _____.

Summary

- The fourth principle of servant leadership is: Servant leaders can risk serving others because they trust that God is in control of their lives.
- The fifth principle of servant leadership is: Servant leaders take up Jesus' towel of servanthood to meet the needs of others.
- Jesus acted out servant leadership by washing His disciples' feet.
- Since Jesus did this for His disciples, you are to do this for those you lead.

Answers to T/F statements:
1. F; 2. T; 3. T; 4. T; 5. F; 6. T; 7. T; 8. T; 9. T; 10. T.

[1]Leith Anderson, *Dying for Change* (Minneapolis: Bethany House, 1990), 192.

Again, here is this week's memory verse, this time with a few of the words omitted. Complete the verse. If you need a little help, don't worry. Simply turn back to page 5.

"For even the Son of Man did not come to be _____, but to serve, and to give _____ as a ransom for many" (Mark _____).

day 4

THEY NEEDED SERVANTS!

"If you don't share your work load, you will damage the foundation of your ministry and quench the possibility of workers expressing their giftedness."[1]
–Doug Fields

Today You Will
- Discover how the early church leaders met a pressing ministry need by involving others in leadership.
- Examine Moses' father-in-law's suggestion to make him a more effective leader.
- Understand the sixth and seventh principles of servant leadership.
- Evaluate your role as a servant leader who empowers others to lead with you.

Meg helps Stacey with the nuts and bolts of the Youth Ministry. Not a month goes by where bulk mailings or special events require added man or in this case womanpower. Meg, a mild mannered school teacher during the day, super youth worker during the evenings kicks into high gear and within a few hours, tasks which were put on hold until the next day find themselves signed sealed and delivered! With the ministry as busy as it is, God has blessed Stacey and the youth ministry with an incredible servant leader whose heart for young people inspires her to go the extra mile.

Write the name of someone in your church who serves like Meg: _____ Have you ever thought of this person as a servant leader? _____ Have you told him or her "thank you" recently? _____ If not, write or call that person.

A Special Fellowship
After Christ ascended to heaven, He poured out His Spirit on His people at Pentecost. The church grew rapidly. God drew people from all races and walks of life to His church. The new believers lived together in Christian fellowship and shared all they had with each other.

Read *Acts 2:42-47.* Complete the following phrases that describe the believers' life together after God poured out His Holy Spirit upon them at Pentecost.

v. 42: They devoted themselves to

v. 43: Everyone was filled with awe, and

vv. 44-45: All the believers were together and

vv. 46-47: Every day they

Two Threats to Unity

The church in Jerusalem experienced great growth and fellowship through the presence of God's Spirit in people's lives. But as the church grew, two internal cancers threatened to stop the movement of God.

Hypocrisy was the first internal threat to the church. *Acts 5:1-11* tells the story of how Ananias and Sapphira thought they could lie to God and still be part of God's work in the church. God judged their actions quickly and decisively. God does not tolerate hypocrisy among His people. The church learned God's demand for holiness. Great respect for God came upon the church *(Acts 5:11).*

Grumbling was the second internal threat to the church. As the church grew, its needs grew. *Acts 6:1* tells how the apostles had not met the needs of certain members in the fellowship. People were grumbling. Grumbling sometimes means that leaders have neglected to address a need adequately. The church did not have enough leaders to oversee the daily distribution of food. The apostles' inability to serve all the members resulted in division and grumbling.

They Needed Servants!

Read *Acts 6:1-6.* What did the apostles suggest in order to address this need in the fellowship? Write your answers below.

v. 2

v. 3

v. 4

As leaders, the apostles saw their role as ministers of the word of God. Their place in the church was to know, preach, and teach the gospel of Jesus Christ. That is what Jesus commissioned them to do *(Matt. 28:19-20).* They also were responsible for the well being of the fellowship. The church had some members with an unmet need. To neglect it would mean division and hurt in the body. The apostles wisely shared the responsibility of this need with qualified members of the church. The apostles turned over this responsibility with appropriate authority to seven members who were *full*

> Hypocrisy —
> saying one thing
> and doing another.

> Grumbling sometimes
> means that leaders
> have neglected to address
> a need adequately.

of the Spirit and wisdom (Acts 6:3). These seven were to "wait on tables" for the neglected members so the apostles could continue to minister through the word of God. *"Minister"* is the same word for *servant* which Jesus used when He said that the great ones among His followers must serve others *(Mark 10:44).* The apostles multiplied their leadership by sharing some of their responsibility and authority to others in order to meet needs in the fellowship.

> **The sixth principle of servant leadership is: Servant leaders share their responsibility and authority with others to meet a greater need.**

The apostles shared some of their responsibility to involve others to meet a need they could not meet themselves. They also shared enough authority for the seven to make decisions so the widows could be helped.

In Week 5, we will observe how Jesus shared His authority with His disciples in order to meet the greater need of world evangelism. *Matthew 28:18-19a* records Jesus' words to His followers: *"All authority in heaven and on earth has been given to me. Therefore go…"* Jesus gave His followers authority *before* He gave them the responsibility of making disciples *(Matt. 28:19-20).* Jesus shared His authority and responsibility with His disciples in order to spread the gospel around the world.

A Father-In-Law's Insight

The principles of sharing responsibility and authority and empowerment are not new. After the Exodus, Moses was responsible for leading the children of Israel to the Promised Land. One responsibility was to make decisions regarding disputes between people. The only problem was that there were millions of people! Moses sat from morning to evening settling arguments *(Ex. 18:13-16).*

Read *Exodus 18:17-18.* What was Jethro's observation of how Moses was leading the people?

Leaders wear out their followers and themselves when they try to lead alone. Too many youth leaders suffer burnout because they think they are the only ones who can do the job. Owning responsibility for a task does not mean you alone can do the task. Servant leaders know they are most effective when they trust others to work with them. Good leaders train and empower capable people to help them carry out their responsibilities.

Read *Exodus 18:19-23.* What was Jethro's suggestion to Moses to meet the people's needs and carry out his responsibility as a leader?

v. 20

v. 21

v. 22

Servant leaders know they are most effective when they trust others to work with them.

Moses listened to his father-in-law. He taught the people and appointed judges over the nation. Moses shared responsibility and authority to judges to meet the needs of the people.

> **The seventh principle of servant leadership is: Servant leaders multiply their leadership by empowering others to lead.**

Moses and Jesus' apostles met a need by sharing authority and responsibility with other leaders. Paul applied this same principle. He commanded Timothy to entrust what he had taught the young church leader to *reliable men who will also be qualified to teach others (2 Tim. 2:2).*

Jesus multiplied His leadership by empowering His disciples with the Holy Spirit. He told His followers that they would *"receive power when the Holy Spirit comes on you; and you will be my witnesses" (Acts 1:8).* Empowerment always comes before mission. Jesus gave His Holy Spirit to His disciples in order that they may have power to witness to who He was and why the Father had sent Him.

Results of Shared Leadership

What did Jethro say would be the result if Moses did what he said? *(Ex. 18:23).*

In *Acts 6:7,* what happened when the apostles shared their leadership with the seven to meet the need of caring for members in the church?

The benefits of shared leadership include less stress on the leader and satisfied followers. The result is healthy growth and caring. Shared leadership also results in more ministry and more focused leaders. Leaders serve by empowering others to lead with them.

Jesus followed these principles of servant leadership when He chose, trained, and sent the disciples out to build the kingdom of God. *Matthew 10* is the story of how Jesus enlisted, trained, and sent out His disciples.

Personal Evaluation

If you are presently a leader in your youth group, put a check in the box that best describes your honest feelings about leadership.

❏ I am tired and drained as a leader.
❏ I feel like I am the only one who can do what I have been asked to do.
❏ Enlisting and training others will take too much time, and my work will never get done.
❏ I am happy to delegate some of my responsibilities to others so they can share in my joy of leadership.

❐ I have been given much responsibility and little authority.

❐ I have been trained as a leader and feel good about what I have been asked to do.

❐ My church has enough trained leaders to help meet the needs of our fellowship.

What needs exist in your group and community that need good leadership? List them here.

1.   4.
2.   5.
3.   6.

Circle the number next to the needs which you are responsible for in some way. List members whom you can ask and train to help you meet this need.

1.   4.
2.   5.
3.   6.

End today's session by asking God to show you how He wants you to lead. Ask Him to show you others who can lead with you.

Principles of Servant Leadership

Principle 1: Servant leaders _____ themselves and wait for God to _____ them.

Principle 2: Servant leaders _____ Jesus rather than seek a _____.

Principle 3: Servant leaders give up personal _____ to find greatness in _____ to others.

Principle 4: Servant leaders can risk serving others because they _____ that God is in _____ of their lives.

Principle 5: Servant leaders take up Jesus' towel of _____ to meet the needs of _____.

Principle 6: Servant leaders share their _____ and _____ with others to meet a greater need.

Principle 7: Servant leaders _____ their leadership by _____ others to lead.

Summary

- The sixth principle of servant leadership is: Servant leaders share their responsibility and authority with others to meet a greater need.
- The seventh principle of servant leadership is: Servant leaders multiply their leadership by empowering others to lead.
- Servant leaders know their value to the group and seek to stay focused on that role.

- The apostles enlisted others to help them meet the needs within the body.
- Jethro helped Moses lead by suggesting that he share his leadership with capable men.
- God wants you to share your leadership with others so they can experience the joy of servant leadership.

[1] Doug Fields *Purpose Driven Youth Ministry* (Zondervan Publishing House, 1998), 203.

Again, here is this week's memory verse, this time with a **few more** of the words omitted. Try completing the verse without looking back.

"For even the _____ of _____ did not come to be _____, but to serve, and to give _____ _____ as a ransom for many' " (_____).

Take a few moments now to write a few statements here concerning what God has said to you this week through this verse, and how His words have become more meaningful in your life.

YOU AS A SERVANT LEADER

How unusual yet how encouraging to find true humility and a servant's heart among those who have a lot of clout![1]

—Charles Swindoll

Today You Will:

- Review the seven principles of servant leadership.
- Recall the events and teachings of Jesus' ministry that are the basis of each principle.
- Be invited to commit yourself to living like a servant leader in the weeks ahead.

You may ask, "How can my experience as a student in a youth ministry prepare me to be a servant leader?" Kelly is a graduate of the University of North Texas and is now using her education in the classroom. When Kelly was a teenager, she attended First Baptist Church in Kingsville, Texas. Stacey met Kelly while speaking at her church during a VBS week. As he hung out with the group he noticed Kelly was a devoted student to the things of God. Mark, Kelly's youth minister and Stacey's best friend, pointed out that Kelly was very passionate in her work for the Lord and was highly involved in the youth ministry. Recently Stacey was talking with Mark and he told him that Kelly is now serving on his youth team at his current church. After hanging up the phone Stacey thought how cool that a girl who was once a student is now serving along side her former youth minister as a team player. Stacey now looks at his youth group with this thought in mind: "How many Kelly's will journey through our youth ministry and impact other youth later in life because they saw the importance of servanthood while here?" Kelly is a servant leader who moved from being served to serving others. You can be too.

Servant leadership is not something you obtain. It is not a position on the company chart you work toward. It is not a career choice, nor is it a degree you earn. You don't gain it after a six-week course on the subject! *Servant leadership grows out of a relationship with the Master who came to serve rather than be served.* A servant's heart grows out of time spent with Jesus and His teachings, and from doing what He said to do. No book, tape, or conference can substitute for your training time with the Master.

Today we want to review the seven principles of servant leadership. You will write them out and recall the events and teachings from Jesus' life that are the basis of each principle. When you have finished the review, you

> A servant's heart grows out of time spent with Jesus and His teachings, and from doing what He said to do. No book, tape, camp, or retreat can substitute for your training time with the Master.

will be asked to make a commitment to spend time with the Master, learning from Him how to live as a servant leader.

Reviewing The Seven Principles of Servant Leadership

As you think back on all you've experienced during this week's study, try to remember the seven principles and write them below. If you need help, re-read the Scripture passage.

The first principle: Based on *Luke 14:7-11*, servant leaders . . .

The second principle: Based on *Mark 10:32-40*, servant leaders . . .

The third principle: Based on *Mark 10:41-45*, servant leaders . . .

The fourth principle: Based on *John 13:3*, servant leaders . . .

The fifth principle: Based on *John 13:4-11*, servant leaders . . .

The sixth principle: Based on *Acts 6:1-6*, servant leaders . . .

The seventh principle: Based on *Exodus 18:17-23*, servant leaders . . .

You as a Servant Leader

Return to the seven principles you have just written. Circle principles which seem to be a part of your life today. Underline the biblical passages that have taught you most about servant leadership. Be prepared to share your answers with the group at your next meeting.

You may be sensing now that this study was intended for someone other than yourself. You may feel that you are not a leader in the church and that you will never hold any position of leadership. On the other hand, you may now be a leader in the church, and this study has challenged everything you thought about leadership. In either case, you are still in the right place. Here's why.

Because you have trusted Christ to be your Savior and Lord, two things are true.

The first truth is: As a disciple of Jesus Christ, you are called to serve. Sometimes God calls you to lead others, but the pressure of leadership is off when you follow Jesus. Service becomes your priority. Any other model falls short of Jesus' example. Leadership in the body of Christ should always follow service. Meeting needs is your most important task as a servant leader.

The second truth is: You were created by God, bought with a price, called out for a purpose, sent on mission. Success has already been achieved on the cross and in the resurrection of Christ. Your success is measured by your service. God created you for a purpose. He bought you with the price of His only Son's death *(1 Cor. 6:20)*. God's only Son has commissioned you to make disciples *(Matt. 28:19-20)* and to be an ambassador for Him *(2 Cor. 5:20)*. With those credentials, who needs titles and headlines!

See, you do belong here. God wants you to serve His people and those who need to know His love. This fact also applies to being a servant leader in your family.

Jesus has called you to be a servant first and foremost. Leadership comes when the Host invites you to the head table for a season to guide and direct others. The training school for leaders in the body of Christ is with towel and washbasin in hand, kneeling at the feet of others.

> *The training school for leaders in the body of Christ is with towel and washbasin in hand, kneeling at the feet of others.*

Personal Evaluation

Prayerfully consider the following statements. Place a check by those that represent your feelings at this time.

___ 1. I never saw myself as a leader, but after this week of study, I believe God wants me to be a servant leader in my church.

___ 2. I have been a leader in the church before, but this study has helped me see my role in a whole new way.

___ 3. Jesus is Lord of my life, and I commit myself to following His examples and teachings of servant leadership.

___ 4. I want to continue this discovery of servant leadership. I make a commitment now to spend time with the Master, to participate fully in the study, to learn to live as a servant leader, and to discover where Christ would have me serve.

___ 5. I am uncertain about what all this means, but I am willing to continue to seek God's will in my life.

___ 6. I don't think I want to continue this study. These concepts are too foreign to me.

Summary

- Servant leadership grows out of a relationship with the Master who came to serve rather than be served.
- When you follow Jesus, the pressure to lead is off. Service is your priority. Success has already been achieved on the cross and in the resurrection of Christ. Your success is measured by your service.
- God wants you to serve His people and those who need to know His love. This fact also applies to being a servant leader in your family as well as ministries outside the church.

[1]Charles Swindoll, *Leadership: Influence That Inspires* (Waco, Texas: Word Books, 1985), 47.

Mark 10:45
You've thought about this verse all week. Now try writing it completely from memory. For many people, memorizing Scripture is not easy. Do your best; check what you have written; and continue to be thankful for the blessing of God's Word now hidden in your heart forever.

Shelby had never led worship before, but he was willing to let God use his talents. Stacey discovered Shelby's gift of musical talent while on a youth ski retreat. He shared a song that he had written with the group, and Stacey could tell his heart was all over it. It was not even a week later that Stacey asked Shelby if he would be interested in leading worship on Wednesday nights. The youth group was saying goodbye to Todd, the current youth worship leader. Todd had taught the group a lot about worship. Stacey knew that he would need someone with that same desire to lead in passionate worship. Shelby accepted Stacey's invitation to lead, and the youth group has since been privileged to have a godly young man lead in worship on Wednesdays. Shelby is currently a junior in high school, serves as the youth worship leader on a church staff that runs over 7000 each Sunday, and is lead singer of a Christian band. Shelby is a typical teenager going through the mountains and valleys of growing up. School, family and job issues face him every day, but he has allowed God to use his experiences with his own spiritual growth and his family's struggles to minister to other teens. Shelby is a servant leader who has dedicated his talents and gifts to serve God's call on his life. You can be too.

This Week You Will:

- Discover a biblical perspective on how God has prepared you to serve. (Day 1)
- Examine the biblical nature of the church and the purpose of spiritual gifts. (Day 2)
- Inventory your potential spiritual gifts. (Day 3)
- Better understand how God can use experiences in your life to prepare you to be a servant leader. Record an important spiritual marker in your life. (Day 4)
- Learn how God works in people's lives to prepare them for servant leadership, and examine your own life to see how God has used your experiences for His purposes. (Day 5)

Let's look at how God has prepared you for servant leadership.

GOD HAS PREPARED YOU TO S.E.R.V.E.

Today You Will:
- Learn how God wants you to use what He has given you.
- Examine how Paul, the apostle, viewed his accomplishments.
- Recognize your achievements in light of biblical principles.
- Learn the meaning of S.E.R.V.E.
- Take inventory of how God has molded you to be a servant leader.

Prepared For Service

Servant leaders know who they are in Christ Jesus. They know how God molded and gifted them for His use. They trust that God can use every experience to prepare them for ministry. Servant leaders do not need a place at a head table to give them confidence. They gladly serve out of the spotlight, knowing that Christ is in control and they are where God has guided them. They trust that God has prepared them to serve for His glory, not their gain.

The world says that you should use all that you are for your own gain. Skill and giftedness lead to success. Success leads to happiness, the self's highest achievement. God, on the other hand, says that He has prepared you for His purposes to bring honor to Him.

Read *1 Peter 4:10* on page 31 and fill in the blanks below:
Each one should use whatever gift he has received to _____ _____, faithfully _____ God's grace in its various forms.

The Bible says to use the spiritual gifts God gave you to serve others. You are to administer God's grace and gifts in your life *so that in all things God may be praised through Jesus Christ (1 Pet. 4:11).* According to *1 Peter 4:10,* the goal of all God's gifts is service to others.

To *administer* means to *steward or manage.* The meaning of this verb *(to steward)* is taken from a noun describing a house servant who has charge over certain parts of his owner's assets. As a servant leader, you are a steward, or manager, of God's grace in your life. The apostle Paul understood his role in this way. He wrote the Christians in Ephesus and told them *of the administration of God's grace* that God gave to him *(Eph. 3:2).* Paul's mission was to take the gospel to non-Jewish people. He believed this mission was part of his stewardship of God's grace. Paul was a manager of God's grace to accomplish God's purposes with his life.

Paul's Outlook On Life

Paul wrote that all he had earned was in the loss column of his life's ledger sheet *(Phil. 3:7-8).* All he had done and gained in worldly terms was worthless compared to knowing Christ. Let's take a moment to consider Paul's attitude about his accomplishments.

> *The goal of all God's gifts is service to others.*

Read *Philippians 3:4-6*. Suppose you were interviewing Paul for a ministry position in your youth group. *Philippians 3:4-6* and *2 Corinthians 11:21-33* make up his resumé. List those items that are most impressive to you.

Philippians 3:4-6   *2 Corinthians 11:21-33*

You now come to the interview. Paul sits down in front of you. You ask him to tell of some of his experiences. You follow along from the pages of his letters. In the middle of the interview, he pauses and tells you he needs to explain something. He tells you what he wrote in *Philippians 3:7-11*. Read that passage now. In the margin, write what you think his feelings would have been about what he had done and who he was. How does that make you feel? Would you still enlist him to serve?

Paul considered everything he gained through his own achievement to be in the "loss" column of his life. The only "profit" item was knowing Christ.

Write some of your achievements below. Do you see them in the same way Paul did, or do you put your confidence in them and consider them gain in your life? Take inventory of your major achievements. Check whether or not you see them as profit or loss in your life compared to knowing Christ.

My Major Achievements	*Profit*	*Loss*
1._____	❑	❑
2._____	❑	❑
3._____	❑	❑

Pause and pray. Ask God to help you see that all you are and have belongs to Him. Can you honestly state that nothing you have achieved or have become is as valuable as knowing Christ? If not, begin to pray in earnest concerning your complete trust in Christ as Lord and Savior.

Servant Leaders Are Leaders Who Serve

Let's use the acrostic S.E.R.V.E. as an outline for how God has prepared you for His purposes. S.E.R.V.E. stands for:

S piritual gifts, those gifts God gives through His Holy Spirit to empower you for service.

E xperiences, those events God allows which shape you into a servant leader.

R elational style, behavioral traits God uses to give you a leadership style.

V ocational skills, those abilities you have gained through training and experience which you can use in service to God.

E nthusiasm, that passion God has put in your heart for a certain ministry to others.

Your relationship with Christ as well as these five areas—spiritual gifts, experiences, relational style, vocational skills, and your enthusiasm—become the raw materials God uses to mold you into a servant leader.

Your relationship with Christ as well as these five areas—spiritual gifts, experiences, relational style, vocational skills, and your enthusiasm—become the raw materials God uses to mold you into a servant leader.

Paul was a servant leader. God uniquely prepared him for taking the gospel of Jesus Christ to all people. Paul's submission to God's leadership and his stewardship of God's grace both serve as a model for how you can live your life for God. Look at what God did to prepare Paul for his life's mission.

Using the letters from the acrostic S.E.R.V.E., match one letter with the sentence below which describes how God prepared Paul for service.

____ 1. God gifted Paul as a prophet and teacher through His Holy Spirit.

____ 2. God used Paul's experiences as a Pharisee to help him understand the significance of Christ's death, burial, and resurrection. God used Paul's conversion experience and call to ministry to place him in a servant leader role as a missionary.

____ 3. God gave Paul a strong relational style that aided him in the trials and setbacks that he experienced on mission.

____ 4. God gave Paul vocational skills to interpret Scripture in order to share the good news. God also allowed Paul to learn how to make tents. This skill served as a way to provide monetary support for God's mission for his life.

____ 5. God burned in Paul's heart a passion for persons outside Israel to know that Jesus Christ is the Son of God.

God prepares leaders to serve His mission. God has prepared you to be a servant leader for His purposes.

Answers: 1. s; 2. e; 3. r; 4. v; 5. e

Match the components of the S.E.R.V.E. acrostic with the appropriate statements:

____ 1. gifts God gives through His Holy Spirit to empower you for service.

____ 2. behavioral traits God uses to give you a leadership style.

____ 3. passion God has put in your heart for a certain ministry to others.

____ 4. events God allows to mold you into a servant leader.

____ 5. abilities you have gained through training and experience which you can use in service to God.

The next two weeks of study will help you discover more about who you are in Christ and how God has already prepared you for servant leadership.

Answers to matching: 1. s; 2. r; 3. e; 4. e; 5. v

Summary

- God has prepared you for servant leadership.
- You are to use all God gives you to serve others.
- You are a steward of God's gracious gifts for His purposes.
- God has molded you to S.E.R.V.E. as a servant leader.

day 2

SPIRITUAL GIFTS-PART 1

Today You Will:
- Examine the biblical nature of the church.
- Explore the purpose of spiritual gifts.
- Discover how every member has a place in the church.
- Define spiritual gifts.
- Review definitions of spiritual gifts.

Servant Leaders And Spiritual Gifts

Servant leaders know how God has gifted them for service in the body of Christ, the church. Servant leaders serve out of their spiritual giftedness. They seek to lead from their God-given place in the body of Christ. The church works best when its members know how God has gifted them spiritually and when all members, empowered by their spiritual gifts, are in places of service.

Spiritual gifts are the key to understanding how God intends the church to function. They are part of God's gift of grace to those who believe *(Rom. 12:3-6; Eph. 4:7,11-13)*.

To receive God's grace for salvation is to receive God's gifts for service in Christ's body.

A spiritual gift is a *manifestation of the Spirit (1 Cor. 12:7)*. It is not a special ability you develop on your own–that is a skill or talent. You do not seek a spiritual gift. However, you should prayerfully seek to understand how God already has gifted you for His purposes.

God gives you your spiritual gifts for a special purpose in the church when He graces you with salvation through Christ. Understanding spiritual gifts begins with knowing the biblical nature of the church.

The Church

Which drawing most means "church" to you? Circle one.

  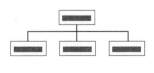

The Bible uses the analogy of a human body as the model for the church *(Rom. 12:4-5)*. The body has many parts, but it is one. The body's many parts have different functions, but together they serve a single purpose. This analogy offers a different picture from the one many of today's churches follow.

Too many youth ministries see themselves as organizations rather than living bodies. Too many youth groups see students as servants to their organization rather than parts of a body. Bodies grow and change. God chose the human body as the analogy of the church because the body of Christ is a living organism. The church is organized like a body, but what it does is more important than who is in what position on the organization chart. The church grows through the power of the Holy Spirit. It functions best when all its members find their places of service.

The Bible describes the church as the visible body of Christ *(1 Cor. 12:12)*. The church is a living body, unified in purpose while diverse in its parts. Each member has a place in the body, and every part belongs. The church is many members gifted by God and united for service.

> *Each member has a place in the body, and every part belongs. The church is many members gifted by God and united for service.*

The Purpose Of Spiritual Gifts

Read *1 Corinthians 12:7* and *Ephesians 4:12*. Why did God give gifts to the church?

Spiritual gifts are for the common good of the church. God gifts members of the church to equip and build up the body of Christ. Spiritual gifts are not for pride but for service. Servant leaders allow God's spiritual gifts to motivate them to serve.

Important to any study of spiritual gifts is God's work in the life of the believer and the church. You do not decide you want a certain gift and then go get it. God gives the gifts *"just as he determines" (1 Cor. 12:11)*. Spiritual gifts are part of God's design for a person's life and the church. The Bible says that *"God has arranged the parts in the body, every one of them, just as he wanted them to be" (1 Cor. 12:18)*.

Your goal as a servant leader is to discover how God in His grace has gifted you for service, and to lead others in the same joy of discovery.

Put a check beside the statement that represents how you see your role as a leader.

___ I see myself as a leader who is responsible for managing a group and finding people for service in our organizational chart.

___ I see the church as a living organism put together by God for His purposes as part of His divine plan. My goal is to serve the church according to my spiritual gifts and help others find where God is calling them to serve.

Everyone Belongs

Read *1 Corinthians 12:14-20*. The Bible uses the analogy of body parts to describe members of the church. In these verses, what harmful thought does Paul address? Look at *verses 15* and *16*. Write these thoughts in the space below.

Some people feel they don't belong in the group or that their participation does not matter because they are not like others. In Corinth, some Christians thought they did not fit in because they did not have the same gifts as others. Paul's response was:

"If the whole body were an eye, where would the sense of hearing be? If the whole body were an ear, where would the sense of smell be? But in fact God has arranged the parts in the body, every one of them, just as he wanted them to be." 1 Corinthians 12:17-18

Every member belongs to the body. Every member has an important place. To feel you do not belong to your church because you are not like those who seem to be more visible is to deny how God put the church together. Every member belongs.

Read *1 Corinthians 12:21-26*. What feeling does Paul address in these verses? Look at *verse 21*.

A member may feel that he does not need others because he thinks his role is somehow more important. Youth groups divide when some students view others as less important than themselves. Someone in your church may think, "Nursery workers with the gift of service cannot be as important as teachers with the gift of teaching." That thinking is not biblical. Paul concluded that members that seem less important are actually given places of honor. He wrote,

"But God has combined the members of the body and has given greater honor to the parts that lacked it, so that there should be no division in the body." 1 Corinthians 12:24-25

No member can say to another member, "I don't need you." God's purpose for a variety of gifts is to provide a variety of services in the group. Just as the body depends on the small thyroid gland for its health, so every member depends on those in "small places" for the overall health of the church *(1 Cor. 12:26)*.

What are some attitudes in your youth group that may cause students to feel like they don't belong? List them in the margin.

What ministries in your youth group may seem to be less important than the others, but in reality are essential to how you carry out the Great Commission? List them in the margin.

The Spiritual Gifts

What comes to mind when you think of a spiritual gift? Write your answer in the margin.

Ken Hemphill defines a spiritual gift as "an individual manifestation of grace from the Father that enables you to serve Him and thus play a vital role in His plan for the redemption of the world."[1] For our study, I will use this definition:

A spiritual gift is an expression of the Holy Spirit in the life of believers which empowers them to serve the body of Christ, the church.

> No member can say to another member, "I don't need you."

Attitudes:

Ministries:

Write your own definition of "spiritual gift" in the margin.

Romans 12:6-8; 1 Corinthians 12:8-10,28-30; Ephesians 4:11; and 1 Peter 4:9-11 contain representative lists of gifts and roles God has given to the church. A definition of these gifts follows.[2] Note we have listed a body part in parentheses beside each gift. These will be important in tomorrow's study.

Leadership (an Eye)—Leadership aids the body by leading and directing members to accomplish the goals and purposes of the church. Leadership motivates people to work together in unity toward common goals *(Rom. 12:8)*.

Administration (an Eye)—Persons with the gift of administration lead the body by steering others to remain on task. Administration enables the body to organize according to God-given purposes and long-term goals *(1 Cor. 12:28)*.

Teaching (the Mind)—Teaching is instructing members in the truths and doctrines of God's Word for the purposes of building up, unifying, and maturing the body *(1 Cor. 12:28; Rom. 12:7; Eph. 4:11)*.

Knowledge (Left Brain)—The gift of knowledge manifests itself in teaching and training in discipleship. It is the God-given ability to learn, know, and explain the precious truths of God's Word. A word of knowledge is a Spirit-revealed truth *(1 Cor. 12:28)*.

Wisdom (Right Brain)—Wisdom is the gift that discerns the work of the Holy Spirit in the body and applies His teachings and actions to the needs of the body *(1 Cor. 12:28)*.

Prophecy (Mouth)—The gift of prophecy is proclaiming the Word of God boldly. This builds up the body and leads to conviction of sin. Prophecy manifests itself in preaching and teaching *(1 Cor. 12:10; Rom. 12:6)*.

Discernment (Ears)—Discernment aids the body by recognizing the true intentions of those within or related to the body. Discernment tests the message and actions of others for the protection and well-being of the body *(1 Cor. 12:10)*.

Exhortation (an Arm)—Possessors of this gift encourage members to be involved in and enthusiastic about the work of the Lord. Members with this gift are good counselors and motivate others to service. Exhortation exhibits itself in preaching, teaching, and ministry *(Rom. 12:8)*.

Shepherding (Knees)—The gift of shepherding is manifested in persons who look out for the spiritual welfare of others. Although pastors, like shepherds, do care for members of the church, this gift is not limited to a pastor or staff member *(Eph. 4:11)*.

Faith (Temperament)—Faith trusts God to work beyond the human capabilities of the people. Believers with this gift encourage others to trust in God in the face of apparently insurmountable odds *(1 Cor. 12:9)*.

Evangelism (a Foot)—God gifts his church with evangelists to lead others to Christ effectively and enthusiastically. This gift builds up the body by adding new members to its fellowship *(Eph. 4:11)*.

Apostleship (a Foot)—The church sends apostles from the body to plant churches or be missionaries. Apostles motivate the body to look beyond its walls in order to carry out the Great Commission *(1 Cor. 12:28; Eph. 4:11).*

Service/Helps (a Hand)—Those with the gift of service/helps recognize practical needs in the body and joyfully help in meeting those needs. Christians with this gift do not mind working behind the scenes *(1 Cor. 12:28; Rom. 12:7).*

Mercy (the Heart)—Cheerful acts of compassion characterize those with the gift of mercy. Persons with this gift aid the body by empathizing with hurting members. They keep the body healthy and unified by keeping others aware of the needs within the church *(Rom. 12:8).*

Giving (a Hand)—Members with the gift of giving give freely and joyfully to the work and mission of the body. Cheerfulness and generosity are characteristics of individuals with this gift *(Rom. 12:8).*

Hospitality (an Arm)—Those with this gift have the ability to make visitors, guests, and strangers feel at ease. They often use their home to entertain guests. Persons with this gift integrate new members into the body *(1 Pet. 4:9).*

God has gifted you with an expression of His Holy Spirit to support His vision and mission of the church. It is a worldwide vision to reach all people with the gospel of Christ. As a servant leader, God desires that you know how He has gifted you. This will lead you to where He would have you serve as part of His vision and mission for the church.

Tomorrow you will learn more about spiritual gifts and discover which gifts God may have graced you with for service in His body.

Summary

- Servant leaders continue to learn how God has gifted them for service.
- To receive God's grace for salvation is to receive God's gift for service in Christ's body.
- The church is a living body, unified in purpose while diverse in its parts.
- Every member belongs to the body.
- Spiritual gifts are for the common good of God's vision and mission for the church.
- A spiritual gift is an expression of the Holy Spirit which empowers each member for service. God desires that you know how He has gifted you.

[1]Ken Hemphill, *Serving God: Discovering and Using Your Spiritual Gifts* Workbook (Dallas: The Sampson Company, 1995), 22. This product is distributed by and available from LifeWay Christian Resources of the Southern Baptist Convention, and may be purchased by calling toll free 1-800-458-2772.

[2]These definitions exclude the "sign gifts" because of some confusion that accompanies these gifts and because they are difficult to fit into ministries within a typical church's ministry base.

As a servant leader, God desires that you know how He has gifted you.

Again, here is this week's memory verse. As you complete today's work, read these words again, and then take a few moments to listen as God speaks.

"Each one should use whatever gift he has received to serve others, faithfully administering God's grace in its various forms" (1 Pet. 4:10).

Now try covering the verse and writing it from memory in the space here. Don't worry if you can't yet write it word for word. By the end of the week, God will plant the words firmly in your heart, and its meaning will grow.

SPIRITUAL GIFTS-PART 2

Today You Will:
- Discover how your spiritual gift fits into the body of Christ.
- Observe how God has put your group together to accomplish His purposes.
- Take an inventory of spiritual gifts.
- Discover how God has gifted you for service.

Spiritual gifts are God's way of empowering members of Christ's body for ministry. They form the basis of how youth ministries should structure themselves to do ministry. Traditionally, youth leaders build an organizational chart showing leadership needs, and then seek out students and adults to fill those needs. Servant-led ministries, on the other hand, seek to build their organizational chart after they see how God has assembled the group or church. A ministry's structure should be open to include members who may not fit into the normal organization of the church. Youth ministries must move from a position where people serve the structure of the church to a position where its structure serves student's needs. Servant leaders lead by serving those on mission with them, empowered by the Spirit's gifts in their lives.

An Analogy Of The Body
The Bible uses the analogy of a body to describe how a church or youth ministry functions best. In that analogy, there are many members, but one body. Every member belongs, and every member has a place of service. But what does that look like? For example, how does the gift of service/helps fit into the church? Go back to the list of the spiritual gifts in yesterday's lesson, on pages 38-39. Remember that there was a body part by each of the gifts. Place each of the gifts in the appropriate place on the "Spiritual Guy" on page 56.

Now that you have completed placing the spiritual gifts on the body parts, you can see how each of the gifts may function in the church. For example, the hands of service/helps and giving reach out to meet the needs of others or do a service project in the church. The arms of exhortation and hospitality bring people into the church and help those who are discouraged to continue on in ministry. The eyes of leadership and administration help the group see God's future and plan to enter into it. The feet of evangelism and apostleship keep the group moving toward the lost and planting new ministries. The heart of mercy helps the group know who is hurting. The right and left brain of knowledge and wisdom help the group know the will of God. The mouth and mind of the prophet and teacher can tell the group how God would have them to live.

> Churches must move from a position where people serve the structure of the church to a position where its structure serves people's needs.

God has given the perfect picture of how He wants the church and your youth ministry to function in order to carry out his mission to make disciples.

Your Youth Ministry As A Body

What would a youth ministry look like if it organized itself around the spiritual gifts of those in the group? When you have completed your spiritual gift inventory, follow the instructions on pages 45 and 46. When you come together at your next meeting be prepared to enter your three gifts/body parts onto the group's composite drawing of the body. When everyone has written in their parts, you will see the gifts that are in your group. This drawing will give you a picture of how you can organize yourselves around the parts in the group. For example, let those with evangelism gifts lead out in planning outreach events. Give those with the gifts of service jobs of setting up on Sunday mornings for Sunday School. Allow for those who have unique gifts to offer what they can do to carry out the mission to make disciples of students in your community.

You can expand this exercise to include all of the spiritual gifts in your youth ministry to see how God has uniquely gifted your group to do the work of mission.

Your Spiritual Gifts

God has gifted you for service in Christ's body, the church *(1 Cor. 12:7)*. His goal is for you to prepare others for service in the church *(Eph. 4:12)*. As a servant leader, you are to use your spiritual gifts for the common good of the body. God gifted you for His glory, not your gain. God gifted you to build up His church, not your ego.

You are about to complete one of the most important activities of this workbook. As you do so, find a quiet place where you can relax, forget the problems of the world for a while, and spend some time thinking and praying about the special gifts which God has given you.

Complete the Spiritual Gifts Survey which follows.[1] Remember that spiritual gifts are for service and meeting needs as part of the church's mission. Every gift empowers members to minister through the body of Christ.

Spiritual Gifts Survey

Directions

This is not a test, so there are no wrong answers. The Spiritual Gifts Survey consists of 80 statements. Some items reflect concrete actions; other items are descriptive traits; and still others are statements of belief.

Select the one response you feel best characterizes yourself and place that number in the blank provided. Record your answer in the blank beside each item.

> When the church worships and seeks God's will, God reveals His plans for different members in the church.

Do not spend too much time on any one item. Remember, it is not a test. Usually your immediate response is best.

Please give an answer for each item. Do not skip any items. Do not ask others how they are answering or how they think you should answer. Work at your own pace.

Your response choices are:

> 5—Highly characteristic of me/definitely true for me
> 4—Most of the time this would describe me/be true for me
> 3—Frequently characteristic of me/true for me–about 50 percent of the time
> 2—Occasionally characteristic of me/true for me–about 25 percent of the time
> 1—Not at all characteristic of me/definitely untrue for me

____ 1. I have the ability to organize ideas, resources, time, and people effectively.

____ 2. I am willing to study and prepare for the task of teaching.

____ 3. I am able to relate the truths of God to specific situations.

____ 4. I have a God-given ability to help others grow in their faith.

____ 5. I possess a special ability to communicate the truth of salvation.

____ 6. I have the ability to make critical decisions when necessary.

____ 7. I am sensitive to the hurts of people.

____ 8. I experience joy in meeting needs through sharing possessions.

____ 9. I enjoy studying.

____ 10. I have delivered God's message of warning and judgment.

____ 11. I am able to sense the true motivation of persons and movements.

____ 12. I have a special ability to trust God in difficult situations.

____ 13. I have a strong desire to contribute to the establishment of new churches.

____ 14. I take action to meet physical and practical needs rather than merely talking about or planning to help.

____ 15. I enjoy entertaining guests in my home.

____ 16. I can adapt my guidance to fit the maturity of those working with me.

____ 17. I can share and assign meaningful work.

____ 18. I have an ability and desire to teach.

____ 19. I am usually able to analyze a situation correctly.

____ 20. I have a natural tendency to encourage others.

____ 21. I am willing to take the initiative in helping other Christians grow in their faith.

____ 22. I have an acute awareness of the emotions of other people, such as loneliness, pain, fear, and anger.

____ 23. I am a cheerful giver.

____ 24. I spend time digging into facts.

____ 25. I feel that I have a message from God to deliver to others.

God gifted you for His glory, not your gain.

Again, here is this week's memory verse, this time with a few of the words omitted. Complete the verse. If you need a little help, don't worry. Simply turn back to page 31.

"Each one should use whatever _____ he has received to _____, faithfully administering God's grace in its various forms" (1 Pet. _____).

_____ 26. I can recognize when a person is genuine/honest.

_____ 27. I am a person of vision (a clear mental picture of God's leading). I am able to communicate vision in such a way that others commit to making the vision a reality.

_____ 28. I am willing to yield to God's will rather than question and waver.

_____ 29. I would like to be more active in getting the gospel to people in other lands.

_____ 30. It makes me happy to do things for people in need.

_____ 31. I am successful in getting a group to do its work joyfully.

_____ 32. I am able to make strangers feel at ease.

_____ 33. I have the ability to plan learning approaches.

_____ 34. I can identify those who need encouragement.

_____ 35. I have trained Christians to be more obedient disciples of Christ.

_____ 36. I am willing to do whatever it takes to see others come to Christ.

_____ 37. I am attracted to people who are hurting.

_____ 38. I am a generous giver.

_____ 39. I am able to discover new truths.

_____ 40. I have spiritual insights from Scripture concerning issues and people that compel me to speak out.

_____ 41. I can sense when a person is acting in accord with God's will.

_____ 42. I can trust in God even when things look dark.

_____ 43. I can determine where God wants a group to go and help it get there.

_____ 44. I have a strong desire to take the gospel to places where it has never been heard.

_____ 45. I enjoy reaching out to new people in my church and community.

_____ 46. I am sensitive to the needs of people.

_____ 47. I have been able to make effective and efficient plans for accomplishing the goals of a group.

_____ 48. I often am consulted when fellow Christians are struggling to make difficult decisions.

_____ 49. I think about how I can comfort and encourage others in my congregation.

_____ 50. I am able to give spiritual direction to others.

_____ 51. I am able to present the gospel to lost persons in such a way that they accept the Lord and His salvation.

_____ 52. I possess an unusual capacity to understand the feelings of those in distress.

_____ 53. I have a strong sense of stewardship based on the fact that God owns all things.

_____ 54. I have delivered to other persons messages that have come directly from God.

_____ 55. I can sense when a person is acting under God's leadership.

_____ 56. I try to be in God's will continually and be available for His use.

_____ 57. I feel that I should take the gospel to people who have different beliefs from me.

_____ 58. I have a strong awareness of the physical needs of others.

_____ 59. I am skilled in setting forth positive and precise steps of action.

_____ 60. I like to meet visitors at church and make them feel welcome.

_____ 61. I explain Scripture in such a way that others understand it.

_____ 62. I can usually see spiritual solutions to problems.

_____ 63. I welcome opportunities to help people who need comfort, help, encouragement, and counseling.

_____ 64. I feel at ease in sharing Christ with nonbelievers.

_____ 65. I can influence others to perform to their highest God-given potential.

_____ 66. I recognize the signs of stress and distress in others.

_____ 67. I desire to give money to worthwhile projects and ministries.

_____ 68. I can organize facts into meaningful relationships.

_____ 69. God gives me messages to deliver to His people.

_____ 70. I am able to sense whether people are being honest when they tell of their religious experiences.

_____ 71. I enjoy presenting the gospel to persons of other cultures and backgrounds.

_____ 72. I enjoy doing little things that help people.

_____ 73. I can give a clear, uncomplicated presentation.

_____ 74. I have been able to apply biblical truth to the specific needs of my church.

_____ 75. God has used me to encourage others to live Christlike lives.

_____ 76. I have sensed the need to help other people become more effective in their ministries.

_____ 77. I like to talk about Jesus to those who do not know Him.

_____ 78. I have the ability to make strangers feel comfortable in my home.

_____ 79. I have a wide range of study resources and know how to secure information.

_____ 80. I feel assured that a situation will change for the glory of God even when the situation seem impossible.

LEADERSHIP	Item 6	+	Item 16	+	Item 27	+	Item 43	+	Item 65	=	TOTAL
ADMINISTRA-TION	Item 1	+	Item 17	+	Item 31	+	Item 47	+	Item 59	=	TOTAL
TEACHING	Item 2	+	Item 18	+	Item 33	+	Item 61	+	Item 73	=	TOTAL
KNOWLEDGE	Item 9	+	Item 24	+	Item 39	+	Item 68	+	Item 79	=	TOTAL
WISDOM	Item 3	+	Item 19	+	Item 48	+	Item 62	+	Item 74	=	TOTAL
PROPHECY	Item 10	+	Item 25	+	Item 40	+	Item 54	+	Item 69	=	TOTAL
DISCERNMENT	Item 11	+	Item 26	+	Item 41	+	Item 55	+	Item 70	=	TOTAL
EXHORTATION	Item 20	+	Item 34	+	Item 49	+	Item 63	+	Item 75	=	TOTAL
SHEPHERDING	Item 4	+	Item 21	+	Item 35	+	Item 50	+	Item 76	=	TOTAL
FAITH	Item 12	+	Item 28	+	Item 42	+	Item 56	+	Item 80	=	TOTAL
EVANGELISM	Item 5	+	Item 36	+	Item 51	+	Item 64	+	Item 77	=	TOTAL
APOSTLESHIP	Item 13	+	Item 29	+	Item 44	+	Item 57	+	Item 71	=	TOTAL
SERVICE/HELPS	Item 14	+	Item 30	+	Item 46	+	Item 58	+	Item 72	=	TOTAL
MERCY	Item 7	+	Item 22	+	Item 37	+	Item 52	+	Item 66	=	TOTAL
GIVING	Item 8	+	Item 23	+	Item 38	+	Item 53	+	Item 67	=	TOTAL
HOSPITALITY	Item 15	+	Item 32	+	Item 45	+	Item 60	+	Item 78	=	TOTAL

Scoring Your Survey

Follow these directions to figure your score for each spiritual gift.

1. Place in each box your numerical response (1-5) to the item number which is indicated below the box.
2. For each gift, add the numbers in the boxes and put the total in the TOTAL box.

SCORE

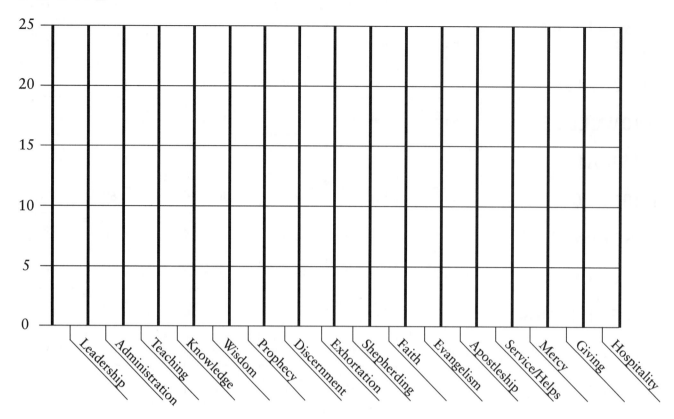

Graphing Your Profile

1. For each gift place a mark across the bar at the point that corresponds to your TOTAL for that gift.
2. For each gift shade the bar below the mark that you have drawn.
3. The resultant graph gives a picture of your gifts. Gifts for which the bars are tall are the ones in which you appear to be strongest. Gifts for which the bars are very short are the ones in which you appear not to be strong. For a definition of each gift, turn to pages 38 and 39.

Now that you have completed the survey, complete these statements.
The gifts I have begun to discover in my life are:

1.

2.

3.

Compare where your three gifts are on the body drawing you completed earlier in today's session. What three body parts do your gifts represent?

1.

2.

3.

After prayer and worship, I am beginning to sense that God wants me to use my spiritual gifts to serve Christ's body by . . .

I am not sure yet how God wants me to use my gifts to serve others. But I am committed to prayer and worship, seeking wisdom and opportunities to use the gifts I have received from God.

End today's study by asking God to help you know how He has gifted you for service, and how you can begin to use this gift in ministry to others.

Summary

- Spiritual gifts are God's way of empowering members of Christ's body for ministry.
- God has gifted you with a spiritual gift to empower you for ministry to others.
- God gave the analogy of the body as the perfect picture for how you fit into the church and how your youth group can function.
- God gifted you for His glory, not your gain.

[1]This survey excludes the "sign gifts" because of some confusion that accompanies these gifts and because they are difficult to fit into ministries within some church's ministry base.

EXPERIENCES-PART 1

Today You Will:

- See how God works in history to accomplish His will.
- Learn how Paul saw his life before and after his conversion.
- Become aware of how God uses experiences to accomplish His will.
- Record an important spiritual marker in your life.

> *Servant leaders trust that God works in their personal history to bring about His plan for their lives.*

The GOD Of History

God is the God of history. History is where God carries out His plans. But God is not just the God of "then and there." He is the God of "here and now." As Creator, God is sovereign over all events of history. Events happen as God either allows them or ordains them to take place. History is what Jesus Christ becoming human is all about. God entered history to save creation from the penalty of its sin against Him. The word incarnation comes from a Latin term and means "in flesh." In Jesus Christ, God came "in flesh." The gospel according to John states that *"The Word became flesh and made his dwelling among us" (John 1:14).* God has always worked in "His-story" to carry out His purposes.

Servant leaders trust that God works in their personal history to bring about His plan for their lives.

Experiences become God's method of molding you into His image. You know what a crucible is from Chemistry class. It is a small pottery bowl that you heat up to make chemical reactions occur in the bowl. God uses events in our lives to heat up things around us to allow "spiritual reactions" to happen in our lives. Servant leaders are confident that events that happen to and around them are part of God's sovereign work in creation.

Paul The Apostle

Look at Paul's (Saul's) life. You have already read his resumé (Day 1). Let's take inventory of his life experiences. Answer the questions as you examine the Scripture passages.

Where did Saul grow up? *(Acts 21:39)*

What were his nationality and citizenship? *(Acts 22:3,25-29)*

Where was he educated? Who was his teacher? *(Acts 21:17; 22:3)*

Before his conversion, what did he do to try to stop the heresy of the Christ cult? *(Acts 22:4-5; 1 Cor. 15:9)*

Whose death did Saul witness and give his approval? *(Acts 7:54—8:1)*

Up to that point in Saul's life, how would you describe God's work in his life?

God prepared Saul of Tarsus for his unique role to carry the gospel around the world to all ethnic groups through the experiences of his life.

- Paul was born a Jew, and he had the rights and privileges of a Roman citizen.
- As a Jew, he knew God's covenant relationship with Israel. He had learned the history of God with His people. He knew and trusted the God of Abraham, Isaac, and Jacob.
- As a Roman citizen, he had all the legal and cultural advantages that position offered. Paul had the best education the Jewish people could offer.
- He studied under one of the leading Jewish teachers of his day. He learned the Scriptures of the Old Testament and how to interpret them and apply them to life.

While Saul did not call Jesus "Messiah, the Son of God" early in his life, God used all of his life experiences as a foundation for what He would do later in the apostle's life.

When Saul heard the followers of Jesus calling this man the Messiah, he began to attack them. He did this as a leader among the people of Israel. His temperament drove him to excel toward his goal. Saul persecuted the church with enthusiasm and conviction. God, however, took all of Saul's positive and negative experiences and used them for His glory. God transformed Saul's enthusiasm to destroy the church into a passion to build it through an encounter with the risen Lord. That is the difference God makes in a person's life.

God And Your Experiences

God can take what has already happened in your life to help accomplish His will. God can mold and make you into a tool of His grace. God can break into your life to make you a new creation for His purposes.

Paul considered his experience on the road to Damascus as the turning point of his life. Each time he stood to tell his story, he told about this spiritual turning point.

Read Paul's testimony in *Acts 22:3-21*. Summarize the events in his life from his witness:

1. His life before he met Jesus *(Acts 22:3-5)*:

God can take what has already happened in your life to help accomplish His will.

2. His experience of conversion and call *(Acts 22:6-16):*

3. His life since his encounter with Christ *(Acts 22:17-21):*

Henry Blackaby, the author of *Experiencing God,* calls events like Paul's conversion "spiritual markers."[1] Blackaby says a spiritual marker "identifies a time of transition, decision, or direction when I clearly know that God has guided me."[2] Spiritual markers remind you that God is at work in your history. Remembering them helps you see God's work in your life and how He is unfolding His plan for your life.

Let's look at the spiritual markers in Simon Peter's life.

Passage	Peter's Spiritual Markers
Mark 1:16-18	
Mark 8:27-30	
Mark 14:66-72	
John 21:15-22	
Acts 2:1-13	

God defined His will for Paul and Peter as they encountered God in history. He will do the same in your life.

A Personal Marker In My Own Life

The summer before my senior year in high school, I went with my youth group on a missions trip. We went to a Navajo Indian Reservation in New Mexico to lead Vacation Bible Schools and do construction work in churches. It was everything a missions trip was supposed to be. We had no indoor bathrooms. We drove into town one day to bathe in the local school gym. I rode with my team for an hour across open desert to get to the village where we held our Vacation Bible School. I remember sharing my faith with a Navajo Indian boy who accepted Christ as his Savior. His horse threw me off when I tried to ride bareback.

On Thursday evening that week, before the revival services we held under a tent, I walked out into the open desert. Lightning and thunder exploded over the mesas surrounding the compound where we pitched our tent. I sensed the presence of God. I sensed that God asked a simple question, "What do you enjoy doing?" I replied, "This. Being with Christian people doing Your work." God said, "Then, go do that." I did. When we got home and shared our experiences that Sunday evening, I came forward to offer my life to the full-time service of God. I changed my plans to attend a state college. I enrolled in a Baptist university and began my training as a minister of the gospel.

That spiritual marker has shaped my life. It helped me to decide what college to attend, what major to choose, and the path my life should take. Even as I write this, I recall the deep certainty that comes from knowing God has a special plan for my life. He cared enough to break into history to reveal that plan to me.

Your Spiritual Markers

You have similar events in your life when God has made His will clear to you. God broke into history, and you know God spoke to you. He may have confirmed a decision you had made. He may have revealed something new about who He is. Take a moment to describe some of your most important encounters with God. You may write these events or tell someone in your study group. If you write in the space below, write as if you are telling a friend about these life-changing moments. Don't worry if you do not have a dramatic desert story. God works in everyday events to shape you into His likeness. Spiritual markers can be anything from a burning bush to a child's gentle touch.

Your Spiritual Markers: Events That Changed Your Life

If you do not have a life-changing encounter with Christ to write about, consider your relationship with Jesus as Lord and Savior. Pause and ask God to confirm His presence in your life. If you know you have not trusted Christ as your Savior and Lord, know that if you will confess your sins and call upon the name of Jesus, you will be saved *(Rom. 10:9-10)*. Talk with your group leader, pastor, or a respected Christian friend.

Summary
- Events happen as God either allows or ordains them to take place.
- Servant leaders trust that God works in their personal history to bring about His plan in their lives.
- God used the experiences in Saul's life to prepare him for his work as ambassador of the gospel.
- God allowed several spiritual markers in Peter's life to confirm His will for the fisherman.
- An encounter with Christ can transform every personal experience for the glory of God.

[1]Henry Blackaby, *Experiencing God: Knowing and Doing the Will of God* (Nashville: LifeWay, 1990), 101.
[2]Ibid., 103.

Spiritual markers can be anything from a burning bush to a child's gentle touch.

Again, here is this week's memory verse, this time with a few more of the words omitted. Try completing the verse without looking back.

"_____ _____ should use whatever _____ he has received to _____ _____, faithfully administering _____ _____ in its various forms" (_____).

Take a few moments now to write a few statements concerning what God has said to you this week through this verse, and how His words have become more meaningful in your life.

EXPERIENCES-PART 2

Today You Will:

- Learn how God has worked in other people's lives to accomplish His will.
- Examine Esther's life to see how God guided her life for His purposes.
- Use a time line to mark your experiences with God.
- Evaluate your life to see how God has used your own personal experiences.

Patsy's Story

Patsy's parents are deaf. But Patsy can hear; and she has learned how to live in both worlds of the hearing and deaf. When Patsy became an adult and a mother herself, she had a desire to work with teenagers. Patsy and her husband decided to move their church membership to a church closer to home. Their teenage daughter wanted to be with friends who went to school with her. One Sunday, a deaf couple asked Patsy to interpret a worship service for them. She reluctantly did so. Another deaf couple learned that Patsy interpreted for worship services. They asked Patsy to interpret for them. She agreed to do so once a month.

Soon a small group of deaf families gathered for Sunday School and worship. Patsy began to meet with and minister to the group regularly. A vital deaf fellowship developed within the hearing church. Patsy did not choose to be the child of deaf parents. She thought at times how unlucky she was to have parents who could not hear. She was not necessarily proud that she knew a second language. Patsy, however, allowed God to work in her life to bring about His plan for her and others.

Today, over 45 deaf adults gather each week from all over the Dallas-Fort Worth metroplex to worship and study the Bible. Legacy Drive Deaf Fellowship has a part-time deaf pastor and minister of music. Patsy did not set out to form a deaf mission as part of God's work at Legacy Drive Baptist Church. The church did not put together a long-range planning task force to reach the deaf of Collin County and beyond. God had a plan, though. He used every experience in Patsy's life to bring about His purposes to create a visible community of Christians who would worship God in their own language and style. God also wanted the hearing and deaf churches to join together to do His will.

Patsy is a servant leader. She served the needs of those who asked for her help, and soon found herself leading. She accepted the experiences in her life as God's design for His purposes. Today, Patsy encourages me by telling me that God will work everything out in His time and for His purposes. I believe her!

> Servant leaders accept experiences in their lives as the raw material of God's work as He shapes who they are.

Servant leaders accept experiences in their lives as the raw material of God's work as He shapes who they are.

As you read Patsy's story, did you experience any common feelings with her?

❏ Yes   ❏ No

If you checked "Yes," what were some of those feelings? Write those in the margin.

Let's look at another person God put in a special place to accomplish His purposes.

Esther's Story

Esther was the cousin of an obscure Jew in exile. She was a stranger in a foreign land. God, however, did make her beautiful. Her cousin, Mordecai, heard about a beauty pageant for the king. The Persian emperor didn't like his wife's stubborn attitude, and he took the advice from his advisors to get another one. The king wanted his pick from all the women of the land. God allowed Esther to find favor with the king. He chose Esther for his wife.

The climax of the story came when the king allowed Haman, a member of the king's staff, to decree the death of all Jews. Haman wanted Mordecai dead because the Jew would not bow down to him. So, Haman decided to kill all the Jews. Mordecai learned of Haman's plan and told his cousin, the queen. He insisted she intercede for her people. Esther insisted she could be killed in the process! He reminded her that if the law stood, she would die anyway. He also let her know that just maybe God allowed her to become queen "for such a time as this" *(Esth. 4:14)*. Esther asked Mordecai and her fellow citizens to pray for her.

Esther trusted God. She approached the king and requested he attend a banquet along with Haman. At the meal, she told the king she was a Jew and that a new law would allow her death. The king went ballistic! He asked who would make such a law that would kill the queen. Esther pointed to Haman. When the king saw Haman pleading with Esther, he thought Haman was attacking the queen. He executed Haman on the same gallows which Haman had prepared for Mordecai. Esther encouraged the king to write a law that allowed the Jews to protect themselves on the day they were to be killed. Jews still celebrate Purim, the day God allowed them to protect themselves and survive the exile.

Esther's story shows how God uses experiences in a person's life to bring about His ultimate plans. Let's look at the events God allowed in Esther's life to accomplish His will. List the experience and how God used each one.

	Experience	How God Used It
Esther 2:5-7		
Esther 2:8		
Esther 2:17		
Esther 4:14		
Esther 5:7-8		
Esther 7:1-10		
Esther 8:8,11		

God used events in the lives of Esther and Patsy to accomplish a bigger plan in history. He can do the same in your life.

Your LifeMap

Your life experiences form a map of God's work in your life. God uses every moment–from your birth and family of origin to the events of today–to mold you into a servant leader for His purposes. You can have hope for the future when you realize God's powerful presence in your past.

John Trent helps you to understand how you can see your life as a map. Dr. Trent suggests that you create a "storyboard" of your life, one much like the cartoon storyboards of animation. He calls the process "LifeMapping."[1]

"LifeMapping is a way of looking at your life by displaying its component parts so that you see key events, patterns, and your potential in a fresh, new way. It involves 'storyboarding' your past and your future so that you become an active participant in rewriting your own life story. And its goal is to move you with clarity and conviction toward closer relationships, Christlikeness, and a hope-filled future."[2]

Dr. Trent asks the readers to consider personal perceptions and significant events in their past and future. The process begins when you discover God's plan for you. Your LifeMap, then, helps you to achieve that purpose. LifeMapping involves both a look back and a look ahead.

Let's stop and take a look at your life. A time line tells history. You learned to do this in elementary school for a book review or history assignment. You simply record the events from the story or historical era on a line that represents years. Let's try this with your life. Mark your birth and "spiritual markers" you wrote about yesterday on the line below.

Make a list of the markers you placed on the time line in the space provided below. Then, evaluate how God has used those events to make you into the potential servant leader you can be today.

	My Spiritual Marker	How God Used These Events
1.		
2.		
3.		
4.		

You can have hope for the future when you realize God's powerful presence in your past.

A Not-So-Childish Story

One of my favorite stories is by C. S. Lewis, *The Horse and His Boy*. In the story, an orphan named Shasta meets a speaking horse from Narnia. They agree to travel together. A creature pursues them throughout their trip home. Events happen that frighten Shasta. He wonders why so many bad things keep happening to him. Shasta declares himself, "the most unfortunate boy that ever lived in the whole world."[3] Finally, Shasta and the creature meet. The animal that pursued Shasta and his horse turns out to be Aslan, the lion and god-figure in the book. Aslan describes each event that Shasta thought was bad and dangerous. Every event guided Shasta to make his way to Narnia. Aslan tells Shasta his story and about his home in Narnia. When the boy and his horse arrive in Narnia, he discovers he is a prince and heir to the throne! Looking back, Shasta sees that Aslan guided him through experiences to receive his true inheritance.

I love this story because it paints a picture of providence for me. God uses good and bad events to guide us to our inheritance in Christ Jesus. God is at work around you. He has been at work your whole life. He has been guiding each of us to our inheritance as children of God. God can use any event in our lives to guide us to His kingdom. As you prayerfully consider how God has worked in your life, rejoice that your goal is secure in him.

God is at work around you. He has been at work your whole life.

Summary

- Servant leaders accept every experience in their lives as raw material God can use to accomplish His bigger plan.
- God guided Esther's life to preserve Israel while in exile.
- You have a LifeMap that shows how God is at work in your life.
- While you may feel that you are the unluckiest person in the world, God is at work to move you to your eternal inheritance in Christ Jesus.

[1]Reprinted from *LifeMapping: Workbook Edition*. Copyright © 1998 by John Trent, Ph.D. Used by permission of WaterBrook Press, Colorado Springs, CO. All rights reserved.
[2]Ibid, 13.
[3]C. S. Lewis, *The Horse and His Boy*, book five in *The Chronicles of Narnia* (New York: Collier Books, 1970), 137.

1 Peter 4:10
You've thought about this verse all week. Now try writing it completely from memory. For many people, memorizing Scripture is not easy. Do your best; check what you have written; and continue to be thankful for the blessing of God's Word now hidden in your heart forever.

Spiritual Guy

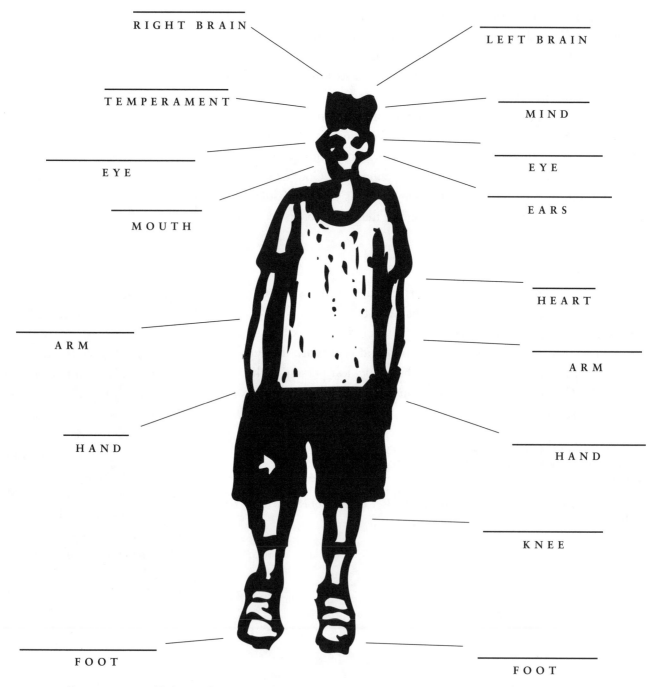

RIGHT BRAIN

LEFT BRAIN

TEMPERAMENT

MIND

EYE

EYE

MOUTH

EARS

HEART

ARM

ARM

HAND

HAND

KNEE

FOOT

FOOT

Directions: Take a look at the body parts on pages 38 and 39. Place each of the spiritual gifts in the appropriate place on Spiritual Guy.

THIS WEEK'S
MEMORY VERSE:

"But he said to me, 'My grace is sufficient for you, for my power is made perfect in weakness.' Therefore I will boast all the more gladly about my weaknesses, so that Christ's power may rest on me" (2 Cor. 12:9, NIV).

Storey likes to have things just right. (She's my oldest daughter.) Once she and I were riding in her car. I wanted to change the CD that was playing so I reached over, took out the CD and placed it in its cover. I then put it in the console between the front two seats. After I had placed the new CD in the player, Storey explained I had put the first CD in the wrong place. She said she had put all of them in specific places, and she asked me to put it where it "belonged." I said, "Well, excuuuuuse me!" and put it where she had designed for it to go. Driving a little farther down the road, Storey said, "Thank you Dad for putting the CD where I wanted it. But, I want you to know I am NOT obsessive compulsive." I laughed out loud. Storey joined in. She may not be obsessive compulsive but she sure couldn't continue to drive until things were in the right place; that is, according to what she thought was the right place!

Storey was simply acting out her natural relational style when she asked me to put things in their proper places. That same temperament allows her to make great grades, plan ahead and hold to high moral standards. It allows her to honor her parents and the things of God because that is the right thing to do. Her relational style allows her to pay attention to details and makes her conscientious. She is often chosen to be the leader because she can be trusted and will do what she is asked to do. Her friends know she is loyal and is honest.

Storey's relational style, however, can drive other people crazy with her insistence to get things "right." She may sometimes come across as inflexible and rigid because she holds to her standards so strongly. Her favorite line is "It's not fair" because she sees things so clearly as right and wrong. Her statements about how things are may come across as arrogant or uncaring. Any strength pushed to an extreme can become a weakness.

God has created you with a unique relational style. You may relate with everything about what Storey does. You also may hope you never meet her! Whatever your feelings about Storey, you have a natural style, too. That natural temperament is part of your motivations and responses to people and tasks. Your relational style is one of the five "raw materials" God uses to mold you into a unique servant leader. How you relate to others also influences how you will lead others as a servant leader.

This Week You Will:

- Discover how you relate to others; overview four relational styles; and identify your own personal style of relating to others. (Day 1)
- Compare relational styles of biblical characters. (Day 2)
- Take account of how God uses your vocational skills to accomplish His mission in the world. (Day 3)
- Inventory the vocational skills which relate to your calling. (Day 4)
- Understand how God fills you with enthusiasm for ministry. (Day 5)
- Complete your S.E.R.V.E. Profile for the next group meeting.

RELATING TO OTHERS-PART 1

Today You Will:
- Consider relational styles and complete the Relational Survey.
- Learn how your relational style affects how you lead.
- Overview four primary relational styles.
- Begin to understand how God has empowered you to overcome conflict through an understanding of the relational styles of others.

How Does Storey Relate?

I told you about Storey in the introduction to this unit. Return to her story and read how I described her relational style. Write a key phrase that describes her style here:

Go back to the same paragraph and list the strengths and the weaknesses of Storey's style. Record your answers in the chart below.

Strengths of Storey's Style	Weaknesses of Storey's Style
1._____	1._____
2._____	2._____
3._____	3._____

Storey's strengths could include a commitment to high standards, attention to details, and being conscientious. Her weaknesses may include perceived inflexibility and being overly opinionated.

Every person has a natural style of how he or she relates to others. Every style has its strengths and weaknesses. God can use any relational style that is submitted to His will to serve His purposes.

How you relate to others is basic to how you serve as a leader. To know your relational style is to know how God has molded you to serve people through your relationships with them.

Servant leaders know how they naturally relate to others and how others relate to them.

Since leadership involves influencing others for the common good, knowing how God has molded your temperament is key to understanding and developing your leadership style. Knowing the style of others also allows you to meet their relational needs. Moreover, understanding the relational needs of others helps you communicate with and lead them more effectively. This knowledge will aid you as you equip others (Week 4) and team with them in ministry (Week 5).

Two words of caution:

1. *Your natural relational style is not an excuse for sinful behavior.* It is not biblical to say, "I'm a dominant person. I tend to run over people.

> *God can use any relational style that is submitted to His will to serve His purposes.*

Excuse me if I hurt you." God's Spirit is the balance to your natural style. This week's memory verse describes how God balanced Paul's self-sufficient temperament. God allowed a "thorn in the flesh" to teach Paul he was not as strong as he thought he was. In his weakness, Paul discovered the power of God. He learned to boast in his weakness rather than in his accomplishments.

2. *To discover your natural relational style does not automatically determine how you will relate in every relationship and situation.* God created you a living being, not a machine. You make choices, and your natural style does not always predetermine those choices.

God will help you understand your role as a servant leader as you assess the strengths and weaknesses of your relational style. The learning activity which follows is designed to help you do this, and is a major part of this week's study. It involves the completion of a survey which will prove to be an interesting and thought-provoking experience.

This activity is based upon a behavioral theory used often by other Christian writers. This four-category model has been proven over time and has strong scientific support. My primary source for understanding this behavioral theory is the guidance and teaching from my friend Ken Voges, who has written a book titled, *Understanding How Others Misunderstand You.*[1] He has written the "Relationship Survey" included here. Voges uses the letters DISC to represent the four primary relational styles.

- **D** stands for the "dominance" style.
- **I** stands for the "influencing" style.
- **S** is the "steadiness" style.
- **C** represents the "conscientious" style.

Here's how these letters compare to other models based on similar theories.

DISC	SMALLEY/TRENT[2]	LAHAYE[3]
Dominance	Lion	Choleric
Influencing	Otter	Sanguine
Steadiness	Golden Retriever	Phlegmatic
Conscientious	Beaver	Melancholic

Plan to spend a little extra time with this survey, completing it as accurately as possible. Also plan to spend some time today (or later on in the week, if necessary) thinking about what you have discovered and how the survey reflects your own style of servant leadership. Ask the question, How does this understanding of myself help me in my role as a servant leader? You will have an opportunity to talk about your relational style at your next group meeting.

Complete the survey as accurately as possible. Some of the choices may be difficult, but do your best to rank each set of terms as they honestly reflect your distinctive, God-given personality. During your group meeting, you will not be asked to share any specific information that you would not want to share. Your ranking of each set does not reflect a right or wrong choice, nor does it assume that any particular personality style is preferable to another. Your results will give you a picture of strengths you possess which you may never have seen before. It will help you to consider how these strengths can be used in servant leadership.

RELATIONAL SURVEY[4]

☐	☐	☐	☐

☐ Forceful	☐ Lively	☐ Modest	☐ Tactful
☐ Aggressive	☐ Emotional	☐ Accommodating	☐ Consistent
☐ Direct	☐ Animated	☐ Agreeable	☐ Accurate
☐ Tough	☐ People-oriented	☐ Gentle	☐ Perfectionist
☐ Daring	☐ Impulsive	☐ Kind	☐ Cautious
☐ Competitive	☐ Expressive	☐ Supportive	☐ Precise
☐ Risk taker	☐ Talkative	☐ Relaxed	☐ Factual
☐ Argumentative	☐ Fun-loving	☐ Patient	☐ Logical
☐ Bold	☐ Spontaneous	☐ Stable	☐ Organized
☐ Take charge	☐ Optimistic	☐ Peaceful	☐ Conscientious
☐ Candid	☐ Cheerful	☐ Loyal	☐ Serious
☐ Independent	☐ Enthusiastic	☐ Good listener	☐ High standards

_____ Total   _____ Total   _____ Total   _____ Total

Note: If your four totals do not add up to 120, you did not complete the survey correctly or you made a mistake in adding up the totals. Recheck your work.

Tallying Your Score

1. If you have not added your scores on each of the vertical columns, please do so now. Then, in the large square above the first column, write the letter "D." Above the second column, write "I"; above the third column, write "S"; and above the fourth column, write "C." Transfer each of the DISC totals from the bottom of the survey to the boxes below.

D	I	S	C

2. Using these totals, plot your D-I-S-C dimensions on the graph shown here; then connect the four points. (Examples are shown in the margin.) This will become your own personal DISC profile.

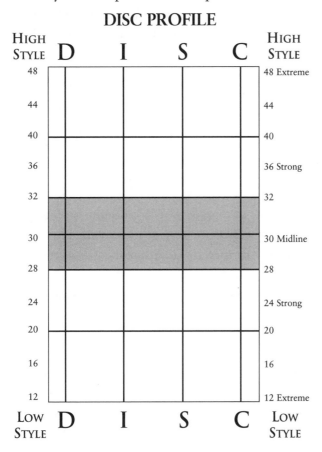

DISC PROFILE

3. After completing the graph, circle all of the points above the midline(30). My High Style(s) are:

4. You will find brief definitions of the four DISC personality styles on page 62. Circle the style which you perceive best describes your personality. You probably have characteristics of each of the four styles, but ask yourself, Which style is most like me? That is the style you should circle.

HIGH DOMINANT

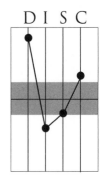

HIGH INFLUENCING

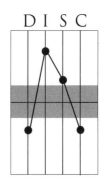

HIGH STEADINESS

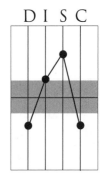

HIGH CONSCIENTIOUS

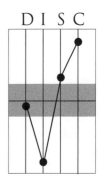

Definitions Of Disc Styles[5]

Dominant Style: Works toward achieving goals and results; functions best in active, challenging environments.

Influencing Style: Works toward relating to people through verbal persuasion; functions best in friendly, favorable environments.

Steadiness Style: Works toward supporting and cooperating with others; functions best in supportive, harmonious environments.

Conscientious Style: Works toward doing things right and focuses on details; functions best in structured, orderly environments.

How does this match what was revealed in your DISC Profile chart? Consider how your survey results are plotted on the graph. Note not only what is high, but also what is low. Ask yourself, Does this information accurately reflect my personality and how I see myself relating to others?

Now, personalize your DISC style by completing the following statements:

- Because of my special, God-given style of relating to others, I tend to work toward . . .

- and function best in . . .

- But I also see these additional qualities of my God-given personality:

The most important part of this survey is a reflection on this question: How does my relationship style relate to servant leadership? How can my own God-given temperament be used by God to make a difference in my church and community?

As you think about these questions, note the following chart which summarizes possible strengths and weaknesses of each leadership style.[6]

Dominant		Influencing	
Strengths	*Weaknesses*	*Strengths*	*Weaknesses*
Direct	Too controlling	Friendly	Not remembering the goal
Active	Hates routine	Enthusiastic	Poor follow through
Decisive	Hates details	Extremely flexible	Overlooks details

Steadiness		Conscientious	
Strengths	*Weaknesses*	*Strengths*	*Weaknesses*
Cooperative	Fails to confront	Detailed	Inflexible
Deliberate	Dislikes change	Conscientious	Rigid
Supportive	Too compromising	Cautious	Indecisive

Note that each style has strengths and weaknesses. No single style can meet every need. God intentionally created a variety of styles, none being more important or more needed than another. All gifts and strengths are important to the overall servant ministry of your church. At the same time, each strength, when out of control, can become a weakness. And weaknesses should not become excuses for failure. A person and a church constantly must strive to accomplish without excuse the ministries received from God.

This diversity of styles within the church may at times produce conflict, but it provides the important balance needed to accomplish what God gives the church to do. It reminds us of the important lesson that *God needs each one of us, and that we need each other.*

Circle the words or phrases in the chart on page 62 which describe you best. This is an opportunity to remind yourself of who you are in Christ and to think about how He can use you in servant ministry. Honestly be grateful for your strengths, and objectively consider the weaknesses you need to overcome.

As you consider this chart, it may be interesting to think about your close friends or a family member. How does God use your different styles to complement each other?

Your Style And Change

Each relational style responds differently to change. Although you are a young person with an excitement about the future, not every person is open to change and differences in other people's lives. Let me give you an example. Stacey and I agreed with the rest of the church leadership that we needed two full hours of Bible Study for youth on Sunday mornings. We had never done it that way before, but the youth group had grown to over 120 on Sunday mornings, and the portable building we had built for students could hold no more. We had to create another place for others to find a place of belonging and caring. Well, needless to say, we got responses to the idea from many people—both youth and parents.

I have found that most conflicts happen in church over issues caused by temperament rather than doctrine or spiritual issues. The two-Sunday School idea was no different. Those who create and accept change (usually D's and I's) were excited about the idea. By the way, D's like to create change. I's will accept it if their friends accept the change. Some I's fear change because they fear the loss of friends. This group began looking at ways to form the new groups, invite new friends, and was the first to jump at the new opportunity. Those who naturally maintain the status quo (S's and C's) tended to resist the concept. S's resist change because they do not like conflict, and change causes conflict sometimes. C's don't like change because it would mean they would have to re-draw their lines of how things work! People with these styles had all the reasons why creating the new Sunday School hour would destroy the youth group. Other factors played into how people responded to the idea, but primarily if you knew their relational style you could predict how they would react to the idea.

> God intentionally created a variety of styles, none being more important or more needed than another.

What do you do if you experience conflict with another person that was caused by different perspectives about change? You remain friends. Why? Because you love the person more than you disagree with his or her preferences. Churches function best when members accept the relational styles of others and seek to meet the needs of those persons, while never compromising the message of Christ. Relationships remain strong when members follow God's pattern for living together as His body with all its diversity *(1 Cor. 12:14-26)*.

God's Word About Conflict

God's Word offers clear teaching on how we are to serve one another in love. *Colossians 3:12-14* says, *"Therefore, as God's chosen people, holy and dearly loved, clothe yourselves with compassion, kindness, humility, gentleness and patience. Bear with each other and forgive whatever grievances you may have against one another. Forgive as the Lord forgave you. And over all these virtues put on love, which binds them all together in perfect unity."*

Circle the "clothing" you are to wear as a chosen child of God.

What should be your standard for forgiveness?

What is the virtue which "binds them all together in perfect unity"?

As a servant leader, you should be sensitive to a person's relational needs and serve him by loving and forgiving as Christ loved and forgave you.

Take a moment and ask God to give you the name of someone with whom you currently have conflict. Seek to understand the differences in relating styles that may have contributed to the conflict. Ask God to clothe you in His love and give you the grace to forgive this person with the forgiveness with which He has forgiven you. Resolve to go to that person this week and seek forgiveness. *"Make up your mind not to put any stumbling block or obstacle in your brother's way" (Rom. 14:13).*

Remember that your natural relational style is not an excuse to sin. God's indwelling Spirit balances your natural tendencies with God's temperament. Regardless of your style, the fruit of the Spirit *(Gal. 5:22-23)* is always a vital part of a servant leader's relationships. God's Spirit molds your temperament for His glory.

Tomorrow, you will complete an interesting activity which will compare your style with that of a well-known Bible personality. You will see how God used this person's personality, and consider how He may also use your style to make a difference in the world.

SUMMARY

- You have a natural style of how you relate to others.
- There are four primary relational styles. Each style has its strengths and weaknesses.

- Conflict happens when people's natural styles cause differences of opinion and/or are pushed to extreme.
- God's Word teaches that you are to be compassionate and forgiving to those with whom you may have conflict.
- God's Holy Spirit is the balance to your natural style.

[1]Ken Voges and Ron Braund, *Understanding How Others Misunderstand You* (In His Grace, 1999). Ken has co-authored a workbook by the same name which contains two personality assessment tests and studies which are ideal for retreats and small groups. Ken is responsible for the biblical content in the Biblical Personal Profile available from Carlson Learning Company. I am indebted to Ken for his insights into the biblical characters portrayed in this unit. Copies of the *Understanding How Others Misunderstand You* book and workbook can be obtained through In His Grace, Inc., 10245 Kempwood Dr., E PMB #135, Houston, TX 77043, (877)744-1201 or your local Christian book store.

[2]Gary Smalley and John Trent, *The Two Sides of Love* (Pomona, CA: Focus on the Family Publishing, 1990), 34-36.

[3]From *Spirit-Controlled Temperament* by Tim LaHaye © 1966 by Post, Inc.; LaMesa, California. Used by permission of Tyndale House Publishers, Inc. All rights reserved.

[4]The "Relational Survey" included on pages 60-61 is adapted from the DISC *Adult Survey* and *Youth Survey* published by In His Grace, Inc., Houston, Texas, copyright 1995. Used by permission. This assessment survey is designed to determine your general DISC styles. For a more complete analysis, refer to the *Understanding How Others Misunderstand You* workbook. Information on training seminars, technical support, and stand alone DISC surveys on relationships, team building, parenting, and conflict resolution can be obtained through In His Grace, Inc., 10245 Kempwood Dr., E PMB #135, Houston, TX 77043, (877)744-1201, e-mail KRVoges@aol.com.

[5]Ibid.

[6]Ibid.

Regardless of your style, the fruit of the Spirit (Gal. 5:22-23) is always a vital part of a servant leader's relationships.

Again, here is this week's memory verse. As you complete today's work, read these words of Paul aloud a few times. Spend a few more moments alone with God, and listen to Him speak to your heart concerning servant leadership.

"But he said to me, 'My grace is sufficient for you, for my power is made perfect in weakness.' Therefore I will boast all the more gladly about my weaknesses, so that Christ's power may rest on me" (2 Cor. 12:9).

day 2

RELATING TO OTHERS-PART 2

Today You Will:

- Examine examples of each of the four relational styles.
- See how Jesus showed the strengths of each relational style.
- Compare relational styles.

Yesterday, you learned about the four primary relational styles. You discovered the strengths and weaknesses of each style and how that impacts leadership. You completed a relational survey to discover your primary relational style. Today, you will compare your style with that of a well-known Bible character. You will see how God used this person's personality, and consider how He may also use your style to make a difference in the world.

Let's look now into the lives of biblical leaders to discover how God has used individuals like you to accomplish His purposes.

Paul: A Dominant Leader

Paul was a servant leader whom God chose to serve Him in a special way. Let's observe Paul's relational style and see how God used and molded it for His service. Search the following passages to see how Paul related to others.

Read *Galatians 2:11-19*. Paul is writing to the churches in Galatia to address the fake teaching challenging salvation through faith alone.

Who did Paul address in this passage? *(Gal. 2:11)*

What was the tone of his message? *(Gal. 2:11,14)*

Do you think there was any room for compromise in his comments? *(Gal. 2:15-16)*

❏ Yes ❏ No

Read *Acts 15:36-41*. Paul wanted to go back to the churches which were established on his first missionary journey. He invited Barnabas to go with him. Barnabas wanted to include John Mark on the journey.

Why did Paul not want to take John Mark? *(Acts 15:38)*

How does the Bible describe their disagreement? *(Acts 15:39)*

What did Paul decide to do? *(Acts 15:40)*

In the margin, describe your perception of Paul's relational style as he related to others. Then list the strengths and weaknesses of his style.

Strengths of Paul's Style	Weaknesses of Paul's Style
1._____	1._____
2._____	2._____
3._____	3._____

Paul's strengths could include his commitment to the task God assigned to him, his determination in tough situations, and his decisiveness. His weaknesses may include a controlling spirit and tendency to ignore people's feelings. God used Paul's dominant style to lead the new mission to carry the gospel around the world.

Sarah, Abraham's wife, is a feminine example of the dominant relational style. She suggested that Abraham take her handmaid in order to have the inheritance of God's promise *(Gen. 16:1-2)*. She also insisted that Abraham remove Hagar and her son from the camp *(Gen 21:10)*.

Jesus: A Dominant Leader

Jesus was the perfect human. In His life, He displayed the positive strengths of each behavioral style. He never violated God's law as He modeled these relational styles. In *John 8:12-59,* Jesus displayed a dominant leadership style as He confronted the religious leaders of His day.[1] The religious leaders challenged Jesus' witness. Jesus confronted their thinking by teaching that they judged by human standards and knew nothing of Him *(John 8:15)*. He declared that His testimony is true because He and His father are one, and their witness is valid. Jesus refused to back down as the religious leaders challenged Him.

Jesus displayed the positive strengths of each behavioral style.

Barnabas: An Influencing Leader

We meet Barnabas early in the Book of Acts. He was a Levite from the island of Cyprus. His name was Joseph, but the apostles called him Barnabas, which means "Son of Encouragement" *(Acts 4:36-37)*. We learn that he had a generous heart and shared his possessions with the church.

Read *Acts 9:23-28*. Jesus had just called Saul of Tarsus to a ministry to the Gentiles. Paul began to preach in Damascus, but he fled to Jerusalem when some religious leaders planned to kill him.

What did the believers in Jerusalem think of Saul? *(Acts 9:26)*

Who encouraged the disciples to trust Saul? *(Acts 9:27)*

What was the result of Barnabas putting his arm around Saul? *(Acts 9:28)*

Return to *Acts 15:36-41*. Read the passage from Barnabas' point of view.

Why do you think Barnabas wanted to take John Mark with him?

Why do you think Paul and Barnabas made such a good team? Why do you think they broke up their ministry team?

Write in the margin how you would describe the relational style of Barnabas. Then list his strengths and weaknesses.

Strengths of Barnabas' Style	Weaknesses of Barnabas' Style
1._____	1._____
2._____	2._____
3._____	3._____

The strengths of Barnabas' personality could include his outgoing nature, his enthusiasm, and his flexibility. His weaknesses might include poor follow-through and a strong need to please others.

Abigail is a female example of the influencing relational style. Abigail, the wife of Nabal *(1 Sam. 25)*, used her natural skills of influencing and gift-giving to soothe David's anger and thus prevented David and his men from killing Nabal. After Nabal's death, Abigail became David's wife.

Jesus: An Influencing Leader

Jesus also modeled the positive characteristics of an influencing style. When He came to the well in Samaria, He persuasively and with sensitivity approached the woman there *(John 4:1-42)*.[2] As she asked about water and where people should worship, Jesus gently guided her to Himself, the living water. Jesus influenced her to trust in Him. He confronted her sin without damaging her already hurting heart.

Abraham: A Steady Leader

God chose Abraham to be the father of His chosen people (see *Gen. 12*). God called Abraham from his homeland and sent him into the promised land of Canaan. As we see Abraham follow God's leadership, several events along the way reveal Abraham's relational style. The first is seen when he went to Egypt because of a famine in the land.

Read *Genesis 12:10-20*. What did Abraham suggest Sarah do in order to avoid conflict with the Egyptians? *(Gen. 12:11-13)*
What does this say about Abraham's relational style?

God made a covenant with Abraham that He would make his descendants outnumber the stars in the sky (see *Gen. 15:1-6*). The only problem was that Abraham had no descendants, and he and Sarah were very old.
Read *Genesis 16:1-6*. This passage describes Abraham's relational style

with his wife Sarah. Who made the suggestion to have a child by Hagar, the Egyptian maidservant? *(Gen. 16:1-2)*

What was Abraham's response to this suggestion? *(Gen. 16:3-4)*

What do these verses say about Abraham's relational style with his wife?

Abraham clearly did not like conflict. He preferred harmony, status quo, and security in relationships. He did not like pain, change, and insecurity, but his trust in God allowed him to overcome these natural tendencies to avoid uncertainties. His willingness to sacrifice Isaac, his only physical hope of God's covenant, proved this fact (see *Gen. 22:1-19*).

This is why, I believe, Abraham was honored in Scripture for his faith. The writer of Hebrews described this man of faith this way: *"By faith Abraham, when called to go to a place he would later receive as his inheritance, obeyed and went, even though he did not know where he was going" (Heb. 11:8).* While Abraham's tendency was for steadiness in life and in relationships, God used him to father the nation of Israel and settle the promised land.

Write in the margin how you would describe Abraham's relational style. Then list the strengths and weaknesses of his style.

Strengths of Abraham's Style	*Weaknesses of Abraham's Style*
1._____	1._____
2._____	2._____
3._____	3._____

Abraham's strengths include a cooperative spirit, deliberate actions, and a supportive attitude. He may be perceived to be weak because he fails to confront others, dislikes change, and is often over-compromising.

Hannah, the mother of Samuel, is a female example of the steadiness relational style. Hannah was unable to bear children. Even under harassment from a rival wife who bore children, Hannah did not retaliate, but faithfully prayed to God *(1 Sam. 2)*. When God answered her prayer, she followed through with her promise and dedicated her son to the work of God.

Jesus: A Steady Leader

Jesus also showed the strengths of a steadiness style in His relationships with others. When the religious leaders brought to Him the woman caught in adultery, He defused the situation by drawing attention away from her to Himself *(John 8:1-9)*. He removed the tension before He taught a lesson. This incident showed Jesus' ability to relate steadily to those who confronted Him without resorting to lying like Abraham.[3]

Moses: A Conscientious Leader

God chose Moses to lead His covenant people out of bondage. God also called him to record the Ten Commandments. God's choice required a special kind of person. Let's look at some events in Moses' life which reveal his natural relational style and how God used him for His purposes.

Read *Exodus 2:11-20.* What did Moses do when he saw an Egyptian beating a fellow countryman? *(Ex. 2:12)*

When Moses fled to Midian, what did he do when the shepherds chased off the priest's daughters? *(Ex. 2:17)*

What do these two incidents tell you about Moses' natural style?

Read *Exodus 32:19-29.* God had led Israel out of Egypt. The people were camped at the foot of Mount Sinai, and Moses was on the mountain talking with God. The people became restless and created a golden calf *(Ex. 32:1-6).* They began to worship it. What did Moses do when he came off the mountain and saw what the people were doing?

What does this say about Moses' commitment to God's laws?

Read *Exodus 34:4-9.* God told Moses He would reveal Himself to him. What did God say about Himself when He passed in front of Moses on the mountain? *(Ex. 34:6-7)*

God revealed these attributes to Moses to balance his own high standards of holiness. Moses needed to know the compassion of God while maintaining the holiness of God. Moses responded in worship *(Ex. 34:8-9).*

Write in the margin how you would describe Moses' relational style. Then list the strengths and weaknesses of his style.

Strengths of Moses' Style	*Weaknesses of Moses' Style*
1._____	1._____
2._____	2._____
3._____	3._____

Moses' strengths include his concern for justice, his attention to detail, and his high moral standards. Weaknesses of his relational style include inflexibility, rigidity, and indecisiveness.

Esther is a female example of the conscientious relational style. Esther became queen after being chosen from among the women of the country. When Mordecai, her relative, told her about a plot to kill the Jews, her first response was to state the rules *(Esth. 4:11)*. When she understood the opportunity God had given her to save His people, she boldly entered the king's presence. God used this woman to preserve the people of Israel.

Jesus: A Conscientious Leader

Jesus modeled the strengths of this relational style as well. When asked about Scripture, Jesus defended the authority of God's word. In a debate with the religious leaders of His day, He clearly stated God's intention in Scripture *(Matt. 22:23-46)*. Jesus conscientiously complied to God's standards of holiness as He taught those who questioned Him.[4]

God Uses People For His Purposes

God used the temperaments of Paul/Sarah, Barnabas/Abigail, Abraham/Hannah, and Moses/Esther to accomplish His purposes in the world. God used Paul's dominant style to face conflict and challenges while on a mission. God used Barnabas' influencing style to bring Paul into the church and to heal hurt people like John Mark. God used Abraham's steadiness to teach faith. God used Moses' high standards to record His perfect Law. God used these servant leaders' natural relational styles to carry out His plan in the world. God also empowered them with His power, His presence, and His Word to do more than their natural capabilities would allow.

God provides people with a variety of relational styles to balance the church's ministry teams. We need each other. God used the domineering Paul and the influencing Barnabas to do His will to carry the gospel of Jesus Christ around the world. Their strengths complemented each other, and those same strengths, pushed to an extreme, caused a broken relationship. The same results can occur in today's church and today's ministries.

A Comparison Of Relational Styles

Now that you have observed the relational styles of Paul/Sarah, Barnabas/Abigail, Abraham/Hannah, and Moses/Esther, ask yourself, Which person's style do I see as most similar to my own? Look back at the strengths and weaknesses you listed for each person, as well as the profiles shown here. The DISC Profiles which are printed here show the possible profiles of these four distinct personalities.[5] Look back at your own profile which you completed yesterday to see how yours matches the possible profile of Paul/Sarah, Barnabas/Abigail, Abraham/Hannah, or Moses/Esther.

God used these servant leaders' natural relational styles to carry out His plan in the world.

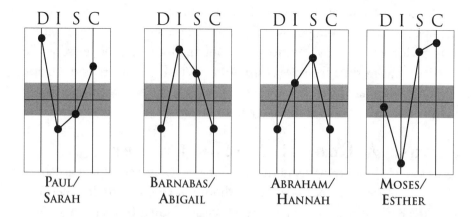

Again, here is this week's memory verse. As you complete today's work, read these words again, and then take a few moments to listen as God speaks.

"But he said to me, 'My grace is sufficient for you, for my power is made perfect in weakness.' Therefore I will boast all the more gladly about my weaknesses, so that Christ's power may rest on me" (2 Cor. 12:9).

Now try covering the verse and writing it from memory in the space above. Don't worry if you can't yet write it word for word. By the end of the week, God will plant the words firmly in your heart, and its meaning will grow.

Check the style most like you (see your profile on p. 61).
☐Paul/Sarah   ☐Barnabas/Abigail   ☐Abraham/Hannah   ☐Moses/Esther

As you reflect on your activities in this workbook this week, remember the following points:

These patterns and interpretations are based on a behavioral profile only—without information about intelligence, personal values, versatility, and other factors that could affect your behavior. Again, no particular pattern is good, bad, or better than another. Knowing your typical pattern should provide you with insights which will enable you to understand yourself and others in a way which maximizes your potential and your abilities as an effective servant leader of Christ.[6]

Summary

- God used Paul's dominant style to further the gospel around the world.
- God used Barnabas' influencing style to build the first missionary team and to restore John Mark to the church's mission.
- God used Abraham to teach biblical faith.
- God used Moses to provide His laws to His people.
- God can empower and provide others in the church to balance your natural style for His purposes.

[1]Voges and Braund, *Understanding How Others Misunderstand You* book, 271.
[2]Ken Voges and Mike Kempainen, *Understanding Jesus* (In His Grace, 1999).
[3]Voges and Braund, *Understanding How Others Misunderstand You* Workbook, 110.
[4]Ibid.
[5]The graphs on page 71 are taken from *Understanding How Others Misunderstand You*, by Ken Voges and Ron Braund. Copyright © 1990, 1995, Moody Bible Institute of Chicago. Moody Press. Used by permission.
[6]See Voges and Braund, 132.

VOCATIONAL SKILLS-PART 1

Today You Will:

- Consider the meaning of vocation as it relates to your S.E.R.V.E. profile.
- See how God used the vocations of those He called to support that calling.
- Assess your vocational skills as they relate to you as a servant leader.

What Is A Vocational Skill?

A vocational skill is any ability you have learned that could be used in a career or hobby. Write one skill you have learned in the space below.

Our English word *vocation* comes from the Latin word *vocare,* which means "to call." A vocation is what one feels called to do with his or her life. In previous generations, a sense of divine calling was part of a person's place in the world. Today, vocation has come to mean any profession, occupation or career. A *vocational skill,* then, is any ability you have learned that enhances your calling or career in life.

In the New Testament, Paul encouraged the Christians in Ephesus to *"live a life worthy of the calling you have received" (Eph. 4:1).* He was not talking about their jobs. He encouraged them to adopt a lifestyle consistent with who they were in Christ. Calling in the Bible is one's position in Christ, not one's position in the world.

Whatever your career, your calling is to live worthy of the salvation God gives you in Christ Jesus. In his letter to the Colossians, Paul wrote, *"Whatever you do, work at it with all your heart, as working for the Lord, not for men. . . . It is the Lord Christ you are serving" (Col. 3:23-24).* Whatever you do, God calls you to live like a child of God and to bring honor to God through your actions. It matters less what you do in life than it does what you do *with* your life.

Church leaders have made the mistake of teaching people that calling and career or vocations are unrelated. Some Christians tend to think of their career as something they do from Monday to Saturday and their calling is what they do on Sundays. Some believe that you are only called to full time Christian service and if you are not called to serve full time, you are not called into ministry. When you read the Bible, you will see that God never distinguished between a person's calling to do God's will and his or her job. Trust that when God calls you to live for Him, God expects your

> *Whatever your vocation, your calling is to live worthy of the salvation God gives you in Christ Jesus. . . . It matters less what you do in life than it does what you do with your life.*

entire life to adjust to that call. Also know that if God calls you to do His will, that does not automatically mean you have to quit your job and go to seminary. God's call in you will affect everything in your life, not just what you do on the weekends. When you begin to see how God can use you in every area of your life to carry out His mission to make disciples, you can become very excited about the possibilities!

Pick one of the biblical characters below. Read the passage about this person's life. Record this person's vocation (what he or she did for a living) and this person's calling (what God asked him or her to do).

	Vocation	God's Calling
Moses *(Ex. 3:1-10)*	_____	_____
Simon Peter *(Mark 1:16-18)*	_____	_____
Paul *(Acts 18:1-3; 9:1-16)*	_____	_____
Lydia *(Acts 16:14-15,40)*	_____	_____

Moses was a sheepherder who led his sheep to food and water and provided them protection. God called him to lead His people out of bondage and shepherd them in the wilderness. Peter was a fisherman. God called him to follow Jesus and become a fisher of men. Paul made tents. God called him to use that skill to support his needs as he carried the good news to the world. Lydia sold fabric. God called her to use her resources to support the mission to the Gentiles.

God called people to join Him in reconciling the world to Himself. They invested everything they had learned and could do to carry out God's call on their lives.

Jesus Was A Carpenter

We don't consider Jesus as a person with a career. However, until He stepped into the public eye at age 30, He had a vocation as a carpenter following in the footsteps of Joseph *(Mark 6:3)*. We can only speculate what Jesus did as a carpenter. Perhaps God used the times of creating needed tools and furniture from unhewn trees to remind Jesus of His power and joy in the act of creation. Mending broken items that were brought to Him reflected Jesus' desire to mend the broken hearts of people. Jesus was well known in His hometown *(Mark 6:1-6)*. This may have been because Jesus kindly went about helping others through His vocation of carpentry. God placed Jesus in the home of a carpenter to teach Him a trade and mold His heart for ministry.

A Personal Story

One of the pivotal moments in my life was when I realized that I could have any job and still live out God's calling in my life. I shared with you God's call in my life to pursue a full-time Christian vocation. I was convinced that God wanted me to be a pastor. My temperament and models for ministry guided me to be the guy up front. After I graduated from college

God placed Jesus in the home of a carpenter to teach Him a trade and mold His heart for ministry.

and got married (in that order), I joined the staff of a suburban church as a pastoral intern. This was ideal as I began seminary. I soon found myself spending most of my time with youth. My wife was a middle school and high school teacher, so the fit was perfect. In 1979, the year I began my Ph.D. studies, this church of 3,000 members asked me to be its youth minister. My wife and church family sensed this was what God wanted us to do, so we jumped in with both feet.

After three years of full-time ministry and as I finished my doctoral seminar work, a college friend called and asked me to consider heading up a private foundation that ministered through camps and conference centers. We had dreamed together about a camping ministry that could help youth in need. Youth summer camp was always the high point of my year. I sensed that God wanted me to do that full time! Again, my wife and church family sensed this was what God wanted me to do. It was a hard decision. How could I be a pastor as God called me to be and the executive director of some unknown, private foundation? I felt I was leaving God's call.

I finished my doctoral degree. I soon found myself frustrated as I taught a Sunday School class with a degree in New Testament studies and hung out with students on ropes courses at our camps. How could I be doing what God called me to do? This didn't make sense.

One day I sat quietly on the side of a mountain outside a Colorado camp. I opened my heart to God. I prayed, "Why haven't you made me a pastor? I have my degrees and experience. I know I can do the job. Why at age 33 haven't you let me do what I thought you called me to do 16 years ago?"

I was really upset.

Then the still, small voice of the Spirit said, "Gene, you can be a postman and do what I called you to do." I listened longer. God's Spirit pointed out that the position I held had little to do with His hold on my life. The Spirit continued, "Be faithful to the task at hand." *Romans 8:28* came to mind. I sensed that God knew how all this was working together for His good. That day I separated God's calling from my career. I did not have to be in my chosen position to be part of God's calling for my life. I realized that God can use anybody in any job to do His will. I sighed a sigh of relief and climbed down the hill to lead a Bible study for a group of high school students.

I eventually have seen my calling and career join. God, not I, decided when and how they would come together. God taught me that whether you are a postman or a preacher, He calls you to follow Him. God's call to follow Him has priority over your choice of careers. But, whatever your career, God can use you to complete His plan for your life.

What's Your Story?

What God calls you to do is made clear throughout the Bible. Lists of godly behavior are found throughout Scripture. In Christ, God calls you to live for Him in every area of your life. God may use your vocation to enhance His call in your life. But God's calling takes precedence over any choice of jobs.

> God taught me that whether you are a postman or a preacher, He calls you to follow Him. God's call to follow Him has priority over your choice of careers.

Write out what you believe God has called you to do with your life.

You also may have chosen a career already. Describe your career choice and why you made it.

Now, reflect upon God's calling and your career choices. Make a list of ways the two can serve each other.

Tomorrow, we will look at the specific vocational skills you have which God can use to enhance His calling in your life.

Summary

- A vocation is what you do to provide for your needs in this society.
- A vocational skill is any ability you have learned to enhance your career in life.
- Calling in the Bible is one's position in Christ, not one's position in the world.
- Calling is God's call to salvation in Christ Jesus and God's call to a special mission in life for His purposes.
- God can use the skills you have acquired as part of your career to complete His calling in your life.

Again, here is this week's memory verse, this time with a few of the words omitted. Complete the verse. If you need a little help, don't worry. Simply turn back to page 57.

"But he said to me, 'My grace is _____ for you, for my power is made perfect in _____,

Therefore I will boast all the more gladly about my weaknesses, so that

_____

_____

may rest on me"

(_____ 12:9).

day 4

VOCATIONAL SKILLS-PART 2

Today You Will:

- Observe how God used two of Paul's vocational skills to further His mission.
- See how one person uses his skills to do the will of God.
- Inventory skills you can use in service to God.

Paul's Vocational Skills

God prepared Paul with unique vocational skills before He called him to witness to the Gentile world. These skills—interpreting Scripture and tentmaking—related directly to God's call for him to be a messenger of the gospel.

Read *Philippians 3:5-6*. Then write your answer to the following questions in the margin:

What was Paul's career before his conversion?

What skills do you think he acquired in this position?

Growing up in a Jewish home, Saul learned by memory important parts of the Old Testament *(Acts 26:4-6)*. He went to Jerusalem to train as a Pharisee. There he learned the Old Testament Law, its interpretation, and how his party translated Scripture into daily life. He learned the biblical language of Hebrew along with his native dialect of Aramaic. He learned to read the Greek Old Testament (the Septuagint). He was trained in debate. He was zealously loyal to the oral traditions taught by his teacher Gamaliel *(Acts 22:3)*. Saul's vocational training as a Pharisee prepared him to understand Scripture and be able to tell who Jesus was and why He came.

Read *Galatians 3:10-14*. This is Paul's argument for justification by faith. How many Old Testament verses did he use in that passage?

How did knowing the Old Testament Law and how the Jews interpreted it help him explain justification by faith to his readers?

God gave Saul the skills to interpret the Old Testament before He made him Paul, the apostle. In his discussion about justification by faith, he quoted the Old Testament four times in *verses 10,11,12,* and *13*. God used Paul's skills and His Word to explain His plan for salvation to all people.

God used a second vocational skill of Paul that aided him in his calling. As a Jewish boy, he learned a trade. We do not learn until Paul was on his missionary journeys that his trade was tentmaking *(Acts 18:3)*. The term referred more generally to someone who worked with leather. It was common in Paul's day for teachers and scribes to have a trade to support themselves in addition to their study and teaching of the Law.

Read *1 Corinthians 9:1-15*. Underline the verses that give a teacher the right to receive gifts for his labor.

What did Paul say about himself in *verses 12* and *15?*

Paul said he had every right to accept money for his teaching. He refused to exercise those rights *"rather than hinder the gospel of Christ" (v. 12)*. In *verse 15,* he wrote again that he had not used any of his rights as a teacher to accept money.

Read *1 Thessalonians 2:9*. Paul defended himself to the Christians in Thessalonica by saying that he didn't take a dime (really, a drachma) from them. What did he do instead?

Paul's vocational skill of tentmaking provided income and a platform for his calling to preach the gospel. He would go to a city, rent a booth for his trade, and reason *"in the marketplace day by day with those who happened to be there" (Acts 17:17)*. Paul learned this skill before God called him. God used that learned skill to carry the gospel around the world. If you follow Paul's missionary journeys, you find that his longest stays were in major trading centers. Corinth and Ephesus both provided the marketplaces and population where he could use his learned skill to support God's call in his life.

God allowed Paul to learn how to interpret Scripture and make tents. Then, God introduced him to His Son, Jesus Christ. Nothing was the same after that meeting. Paul's career skills became tools to do the work of God.

A Present-Day Story

Greg has been our church's Youth Associate for over two years. The position was traditionally a "gopher" but evolved into something more. When we found Greg he had just finished his second year as a Centrifuge camp pastor. Greg was travelling around the country, speaking at youth retreats and revivals, and was looking for a place to plug into while he was travelling. "Great," we thought, "here's a guy who can speak on Wednesdays, do random office stuff during the week and still do his speaking thing on the weekends." It was perfect for both of us. I had no idea what God had given our ministry.

Greg is a mesmerizing speaker. I have never seen anyone who can capture an audience, regardless of the size, like him. He does it with stories. Greg takes stories and wraps you up in them. Our kids love them. He'll say "I've got a story for you," and our kids go crazy. Greg has been gifted as one of the best speakers around, with a tremendous gift of storytelling, and that is how he serves. Using that skill, he has transformed our Wednesday nights into something that the students don't want to miss. The Bible becomes real and our students grow, all because Greg uses his trained gift of story telling to lead people into the presence of God.

We believe that you can invest any skill you have learned in your life into the work of God. Some of the best ministries in our church came from people who invested their skills into God's mission to make disciples. Our English as a Second Language Class began when Janet said she wanted to teach ESL at our church so she could use the Bible as a textbook. Our Skills and Drills Basketball camp began when Billy stepped forward to offer his skills of basketball instruction to the work of God. Our church's best ministries have been started by people who were willing to invest what they had learned as a tool to reach others.

Your Vocational Skills

Vocational skills are those skills you have acquired to do a job and/or hobby. Let's make an inventory of your skills. Use the table below to create your skill inventory:

Name of Skill	How I Use This Skill in My Vocation
1.	
2.	
3.	

Your Skills For God's Calling

God used Paul's vocational skills of making tents and interpreting Scriptures for his life's calling. God can do the same for you. Now that you have inventoried your major skills, take time to imagine how God can use those skills for His work of spreading the gospel through your church or organization's ministry to youth.

For example, if one of your skills is building websites, you can use that skill to build a website for your youth group on the world wide web. If you like writing, you may write stories for a youth newsletter and let friends who can do publishing on their computer design it and print it for the youth group. Be creative as you consider how you can use your skills for the glory of God. Remember the words of Paul the tent maker turned missionary, "…*whatever you do, do it all for the glory of God*" (1 Cor. 10:31).

Name of Skill	How God Can Use This Skill in His Mission
1.	
2.	
3.	

Summary

- God prepared Paul with unique vocational skills before He called him to witness to the Gentile world.
- Paul's vocational training as a Pharisee prepared him to handle Scripture to tell who Jesus was and why He came.
- Paul's vocational skill of tentmaking provided income and a platform for his calling to preach the gospel.
- Like Paul, your skills can be transformed to the service of God.

Again, here is this week's memory verse, this time with a few more of the words omitted. Try completing the verse without looking back.

"*But he said to_____, 'My grace is _____ for you, for my _____ is made perfect in _____.' Therefore I will boast all the more gladly about my _____, so that _____ _____ may rest on_____*" (_____).

Take a few moments now to write a few statements above concerning what God has said to you this week through this verse, and how His words have become more meaningful in your life.

ENTHUSIASM

Today You Will:

- Define enthusiasm and see how it relates to you as a servant leader.
- See the role enthusiasm played in the life of Apollos.
- See how John the Baptist modeled biblical passion and the principle of servant leadership.
- Complete your S.E.R.V.E. Profile.

Have you ever met someone who was truly excited about what he was doing? You know nothing seemed to get him down. He was eager to do his job, and you could sense it. Enthusiasm means an intense or eager interest. You may say, "Jeff is enthusiastic about the music he plays in the band. He must love to do that." Enthusiastic people make service enjoyable.

Make a list of enthusiastic students you know. Then answer the question: What is it about their behavior that signals enthusiasm?

	Enthusiastic Students I Know	*How they act…*
1.	_____	_____
2.	_____	_____
3.	_____	_____

The word *enthusiasm* comes from a Greek word that literally means, "in god." The Greeks believed that a god could enter a person and inspire or enthuse him. Our word *enthusiasm* takes on the meaning, "God in you." While the Greek word for enthuse is not found in the New Testament, the emphasis on God's presence which energizes the believer is a recurring theme *(John 14:20; 20:21-22; Matt. 28:18-20; Acts 1:8).* The Bible is clear that God's Holy Spirit is the source of passion for God's mission within the believer. Paul declared it is "Christ in you" which is *"the hope of glory" (Col. 1:27).* We do not generate hope on our own. God energizes us with His living Holy Spirit. Jesus promised that the Holy Spirit will be our Counselor and *"guide you into all truth" (John 16:7,13).* He is our counselor and guide as we follow the Lord. Passion and enthusiasm for ministry come from God.

Scripture tells about people who were enthusiastic about what they did. This is not a self-generated thrill. As it relates to this study, *enthusiasm* is a God-given desire to serve Him by meeting the needs of others. Servant leaders have a God-given passion to serve. Today, we will observe three persons who were servant leaders and enthusiastic about their service to God. We also will see how they differed in their passion for God's work.

> *Servant leaders have a God-given passion to serve.*

> *We do not generate hope on our own. God energizes us with His living Holy Spirit.*

Jesus: An Enthusiastic Leader

Jesus was filled with a confidence and enthusiasm about His ministry. People were drawn to Him because of His passion for life and for ministry. Jesus taught with enthusiasm. The Bible states that after the Sermon on the Mount, *"the crowds were amazed at his teaching, because he taught as one who had authority" (Matt. 7:28-29)*. We get a glimpse of His passion for His disciples as He tells them, *" 'Do not let your hearts be troubled. Trust in God; trust also in me' " (John 14:1)*. We see His all-consuming passion to do God's will when He declares, *" 'For I have come down from heaven not to do my will but to do the will of him who sent me. And this is the will of him who sent me, that I shall lose none of all that he has given me, but raise them up at the last day' " (John 6:38-39)*. Jesus was filled with a passion about His mission, and it showed!

Apollos: A Passionate Teacher

Read *Acts 18:24-26*. Where was Apollos from? *(Acts 18:24)*

How does the Bible describe his skills and enthusiasm?

Apollos came from the intellectual center of Alexandria in Egypt. This city was the home of the Greek translation of the Old Testament. Luke tells us that Apollos was *"a learned man, with a thorough knowledge of the Scriptures" (Acts 18:24)*. He had been taught in the way of the Lord. He spoke with great fervor. The Bible says he accurately taught about Jesus, but his teaching was incomplete. He knew only the baptism of John, a baptism of repentance.

The phrase that described his teaching, "with great fervor," is a translation of the idiom "to boil in the spirit."[1] Apollos loved to teach about Jesus. He boldly preached about Jesus in Ephesus, where Paul had left Priscilla and Aquila.

By itself, however, Apollos' enthusiasm did not lend itself to an effective ministry of the gospel. He knew only of the baptism of John. His passion was full, but his facts were not straight. Proverbs warns, *"It is not good to have zeal without knowledge" (Prov. 19:2)*. Enthusiasm alone does not make you a servant leader. Luke tells us that Priscilla and Aquila took Apollos into their home and *"explained to him the way of God more adequately" (Acts 18:26)*. What the two more mature Christians did is called mentoring. (We'll talk about this in Week 5.) A Christlike spirit, a deep desire to learn, and a servant heart must accompany passion.

John The Baptist: A Passionate Servant Leader

Read *John 3:22-30*. What does *verse 23* say about the success of John's ministry?

> *Enthusiasm alone does not make you a servant leader.*

Some of John's disciples came to him and pointed to the success of another. What did they say to John? *(John 3:26)*

Write the different parts of John's reply in the spaces below.

v. 27 A man can . . .

v. 28 I am not the Christ . . .

v. 29 The friend who attends the bridegroom . . . is full of . . .

v. 30 He must . . .

John first noted that success comes only from God *(John 3:27)*. If people were swarming to Jesus, it was part of God's plan. John also re-stated the fact that he was not the Messiah. He was sent ahead of God's chosen one to prepare the way of the Lord *(John 3:28)*. Then John drew an analogy from everyday life. He said that only the bridegroom gets the bride. The friend who attends the bridegroom is usually the groom's best friend. His joy and job is complete when he leads the bride to the bridegroom *(John 3:29)*. John said his joy was complete because people were being drawn to Jesus. He concluded by sharing the true joy of a servant leader. He said, " *'He must become greater; I must become less' " (John 3:30)*.

John was full of joy because God was accomplishing His will right before his eyes! He knew his place was second chair to the one God sent to bring the song of salvation to all people. A servant leader's greatest joy comes when he sees God at work, and he is part of it. Servant leadership is a God-given passion for the success of God's plan.

Servant leaders find joy when God's will is done. Servant leaders know they must become less and Christ must become greater. This attitude is consistent with the first and second principles of servant leadership, which are:

1. Servant leaders humble themselves and wait for God to exalt them.
2. Servant leaders follow Jesus rather than seek a position.

John's joy was different from Apollos' enthusiasm. Apollos had passion without knowing all the facts. John, on the other hand, had true joy because he saw God's plan for his life being completed right before him.

An Important Note: Your God-given enthusiasm is sometimes your only source of joy in ministry. As you lead, you will face obstacles and disappointments. Other students may criticize you. Sometimes they may question your motives. But the sincere desire to know God's will and the passion God puts in your heart for His work absorb these negative reactions and allow you to move forward with your ministry. Your enthusiasm is the beginning of a fruitful life in Christ.

Your Enthusiasm

What has God burned in your heart to do for His mission on earth? Take a moment to consider what that may be. Prayerfully write your responses to the following statements. Complete them with honest, heartfelt statements. The one thing I do for God that makes my heart beat fast is . . .

If I could do one thing for God, it would be to . . .

Summary

- *Enthusiasm* in our study is a God-given desire to serve God by meeting the needs of others.
- Enthusiasm alone does not make you a servant leader.
- Your God-given enthusiasm is sometimes your only source of joy in ministry.
- Your enthusiasm is the beginning of a fruitful life in Christ.
- Servant leaders find joy when God's will is done. Servant leaders know they must become less and Christ must become greater.

Turn to the S.E.R.V.E. Profile on page 84. Complete each section of the profile from the information you have gained from these two weeks of study. Be prepared to share these insights with your group at your next meeting.

[1]Louw and Nida, *Greek-English Lexicon of the New Testament based on Semantic Domains* (United Bible Society, 1988), 1:297, 8.

> *What has God burned in your heart to do for His mission on earth?*

> *2 Corinthians 12:9*
> You've thought about this verse all week. Now try writing it completely from memory. For many people, memorizing Scripture is not easy. Do your best; check what you have written; and continue to be thankful for the blessing of God's Word now hidden in your heart forever.

MY S.E.R.V.E. PROFILE

Believing God has prepared me for servant leadership, I am discovering that He has molded me in the following areas:

- God has gifted me with the spiritual gifts of (see p. 46):

- God has allowed these experiences to guide me for His purposes (see p. 54):

- God has created me to relate most often to others naturally in this way (see p. 61):

- God has given me the opportunities to develop these vocational skills that can be used in His service (see p. 79):

- God has burned in my heart the enthusiasm to serve in this area of ministry (see p. 83):

I commit these gifts, talents, and abilities to God and His kingdom's service.

Signed_____ Date _____

You have been asked to lead your youth group in reaching students on their school campus. This is part of your ministry's mission to make disciples of every student in your community. You soon realize you can't do the job alone. The task is too big for one person. But, your heart is tugged to reach students who will not come first to your church group. What do you do? How do you get others to join you? What do you tell them to do if they want to join you in reaching other students? Once others are in the schools, how do you keep them motivated and excited as you are? Where does the power of God come from to do something like this? These and other questions will arise when you make yourself a servant to what God calls you to do, and you realize the job is too big for you to do by yourself.

Up to this point you have studied how Jesus taught and modeled servant leadership. You have spent time discovering how God has molded you into a unique servant leader by completing your S.E.R.V.E. Profile. This week you will begin to answer the question, "How do I lead by serving those on mission with me?" Remember we learned in the introduction that servant leadership begins when you become a servant to the mission call of God on your life. When you have committed yourself to completing God's work in your life, you become a leader who serves those on that mission with you. Weeks 4 and 5 tell how you serve those who have joined you on mission by equipping them and building them into a team.

This week you will discover five steps to equip others. You will observe how Jesus equipped His closest followers to carry out his call to mission on their lives. And you will examine other biblical examples of how leaders trained others to carry out the mission of the church.

Here's an explanation of the biblical concept of equipping from my book *Jesus On Leadership*:

The word "to equip" gets its meaning from two different contexts in New Testament times. One was the medical world. To equip meant to set a broken bone in order to prepare it for healing. In that context, it meant "to put in order." The second context was the fishing industry of Jesus' day. Fisherman would "equip" their nets at the end of a casting period. They would restore the net to its former condition and allow the sun to dry it in its designed position. In this way they prepared the net for casting.

These two pictures provide leaders with images of their job. To equip the church is to prepare its members to perform their part of the mission. If the church were a net, the leader's job would be to prepare that net for its next cast.[1]

Reaching students on campus is one way to "cast the net." If you are a servant leader to that mission, your first job is to equip those who join you on this mission to be an effective net to reach others. How you do that is the content of this week's study.

This Week You Will:

• Understand the need to Encourage others to serve in the body of Christ. (Day 1)

• See how to Qualify persons you encourage to join you in service. (Day 2)

• Seek to Understand the needs of those you equip for service. (Day 3)

• Discover areas in which you can Instruct those you equip. (Day 4)

• Know that Prayer is your most powerful tool to lead and equip others. (Day 5)

THIS WEEK'S MEMORY VERSE

"It was he who gave some to be apostles, some to be prophets, some to be evangelists, and some to be pastors and teachers, to prepare God's people for works of service, so that the body of Christ may be built up" (Eph. 4:11-12, NIV).

ENCOURAGE THEM TO SERVE

Today You Will:

- Learn how it is your responsibility as a servant leader to E.Q.U.I.P. others for ministry.
- Observe how Jesus encouraged His disciples in ministry.
- See how Barnabas encouraged Paul to help him meet a need in Antioch.
- Consider people you can encourage to join you in ministry.

Jeni (pronounced Gin-eye) serves as our church's youth publications director. She is a top-notch devoted servant who puts her whole heart into the ministry. Nothing is more evident of that than when VBS rolls around. Over the past several years Jeni has become known as the CEO of VBS at Legacy Drive Baptist. In the summer of 1997, Jeni orchestrated over 100 adult leaders along with approximately 60 youth assistants and ministered to over 400 children. What made this all possible? Jeni knew the power of equipping others to do the ministry. Had she relied on herself and a few close friends to minister to over 400 children, you might be reading about her in the latest edition of, "VBS Burnout, Putting out the Flames." Jeni understands the model of equipping; after all, many touches many and few touch few.

You have servant leaders like Jeni in your church. Before you read further, write the names of servant leaders like our VBS director in the margin.

Servant leaders know it is their responsibility to equip others for service. Servant leaders refuse to think they are the only leaders capable of serving God's mission. Ken Hemphill, President of Southwestern Seminary, has noted that, "Every member of the body is a leader; some simply have more responsibility."[2] Your first job as leader is to discover and identify persons who are ready for service. You are also to equip other leaders to serve with you to complete the mission of God. The church functions best when two things occur: (1) when members know how God has molded them; and (2) when members are equipped for the ministry (or ministries) they have been prepared to do.

Equipping others for service follows the sixth principle of servant leadership: "Servant leaders share their responsibility and authority with others to meet a greater need."

The First Step To E.Q.U.I.P.

Servant leaders encourage others to become involved on mission with them. They know the joy of finding their place of service and want others to share that joy. Servant leaders know that a person who is not involved in ministry is missing out on part of God's plan for his or her life.

> The church functions best when two things occur:
> (1) when members know how God has molded them; and
>
> (2) when members are equipped for the ministry (or ministries) they have been prepared to do.

The first step to E.Q.U.I.P. others for service is to Encourage them to become involved in ministry.

To *encourage* means literally to "call to one's side." You encourage others when you stand alongside them for a time to comfort and assist.

Jesus Encouraged His Disciples

Jesus called the twelve to follow Him to the cross and to be His witnesses throughout the world. He spent much of His time encouraging them. *John 14* contains some of Jesus' most encouraging words to His followers. His disciples were concerned for themselves and their Master. The closer they came to Jerusalem, the more troubled they became about what would happen to them and to Him.

Read *John 14:1-4*. What did Jesus say to encourage His followers?

Read *John 14:5-7*. Thomas asked the question which may have been on all their minds: How can we know the way? How did Jesus' response encourage His followers?

Read *John 14:12-14*. What did Jesus promise His followers?

How do you think this encouraged them to join Him in ministry?

How do these promises make you feel?

Jesus said He would send another Counselor to be with them forever. Another name for the Holy Spirit of God is "Encourager" *(John 14:16).*[3] Jesus said He would not leave His disciples as orphans. He would send His Holy Spirit to be with them. Jesus knew His followers would need His presence to guide and encourage them in the future. Jesus equipped His closest followers by encouraging them to count on His power while they served.

Barnabas Encouraged Paul

Read *Acts 11:19-24*. You have already met Barnabas in Week 3. What were Barnabas' spiritual gifts?

What was his relational style? (Week 3, Day 2, see pages 67-68.)

Jesus equipped His closest followers by encouraging them to count on His power while they served.

The church in Jerusalem heard about what was happening in Antioch, how the Lord's hand was on the church there, and that a *"great number of people believed and turned to the Lord" (Acts 11:21)*. The church sent Barnabas to Antioch. What does *verse 23* say Barnabas did when he saw the evidence of the grace of God upon the people?

The Bible states that Barnabas was *"a good man, full of the Holy Spirit and faith."* God used him to bring many people to the Lord *(Acts 11:24)*. Barnabas was a servant leader.

Read *Acts 11:25-26*. As the church in Antioch grew in number, a need arose for good teaching. The new converts needed teaching that would ground them in their walk with the Lord. Barnabas recognized this need.

What did he do in response? *(Acts 11:25-26)*

What did Barnabas and Saul do together? *(Acts 11:26)*

Barnabas saw a need in the young church at Antioch. The many new converts needed strong, biblical teaching. Barnabas knew Saul of Tarsus was an experienced teacher of the Scriptures. Barnabas traveled to Tarsus and encouraged the Pharisee-turned-Christian to come with him and help meet a need for teaching new Christians. Barnabas met a need in the young church at Antioch by encouraging Saul to join him in a teaching ministry.

Read again *Acts 11:26*. How long does the Bible say the two taught with the people? How do you think this impacted the church?

> Servant leaders encourage others to join them in ministry.

Barnabas was a servant leader who encouraged Saul to join him in ministry. This same Saul soon became the greatest missionary the church has ever known. Paul knew the importance of encouragement. He told the Christians in Thessalonica on two different occasions to encourage one another *(1 Thess. 4:18; 5:11)*.

The church has always had men and women like Barnabas. They never lead alone. They equip others to serve with them in ministry. Jeni is like Barnabas. She saw a need to teach children in VBS. She encouraged others to join in that ministry. Servant leaders encourage others to join them in ministry.

Jesus modeled how you can encourage others in ministry by reminding them of His power and presence in their lives.

Personal Evaluation

As you consider your role as someone who should encourage others to take up a place of ministry, prayerfully answer the following questions:

1. What did Jesus say to His disciples that is most encouraging to you?

2. You may have had someone like Barnabas in your life. This person came to you and invited you to join him or her in a ministry that eventually led you to a place of service. If you have now or have had such a person in your life, write this person's name here. State what he or she asked you to do that moved you into ministry.

3. You may be serving in a leadership position now. Write the names of one or two people you know whom you could encourage to join you in your ministry.

4. What do you see in them that makes you believe they are ready for service? List those qualities here.

5. As you consider encouraging others to find a place of ministry, evaluate your own life. Is there anything in your life that would cause another person not to accept your invitation for service? *Proverbs 27:19* states, *"A man's heart reflects the man."* What does your heart reflect to others? Think about that question for a moment, and prayerfully write your answers in the margin.

Summary

- Turn your attention to those you can equip for ministry.
- The first step to E.Q.U.I.P. someone for service is to encourage him or her to become involved in ministry.
- Jesus modeled how you can encourage others in ministry by reminding them of His power and presence in their lives.
- Barnabas met a need in the young church at Antioch by encouraging Saul to join him in a teaching ministry.
- Servant leaders know the joy of service and encourage others to become involved in ministry.

[1]Gene Wilkes, *Jesus on Leadership* (Nashville: LifeWay Press, 1998), 186.
[2]Ken Hemphill, *The Antioch Effect* (Nashville: Broadman & Holman, 1994), 84.
[3]The King James Version reads, "Comforter"; the NIV, "Counselor"; and the NASB, "Helper." All three translations come from the same Greek word which means, "one who appears in another's behalf" (Arndt/Gingrich).

Again, here is this week's memory verse. As you complete today's work, read these words of Paul aloud a few times. Spend a few more moments alone with God, and listen to Him speak to your heart concerning servant leadership.

"It was he who gave some to be apostles, some to be prophets, some to be evangelists, and some to be pastors and teachers, to prepare God's people for works of service, so that the body of Christ may be built up" (Eph. 4:11-12).

QUALIFY THEM FOR SERVICE

Today You Will:

- Learn the second step to E.Q.U.I.P. others.
- Understand the meaning of qualify as applied to equipping others.
- Observe how Jesus qualified those who wanted to follow Him.
- Examine how Paul taught Timothy to qualify others for ministry.
- Evaluate how you can qualify those you have encouraged.

> *Encouragement without training is like enthusiasm without direction.*

To encourage someone to get involved in ministry is not enough. Encouragement without training is like enthusiasm without direction: you move around a lot, but little gets done! Servant leaders guide those they encourage to join them in ministry. Jesus did not say, "I will make you fishers of men," and then leave Simon and Andrew to figure things out on their own. He invested the next three years of His life equipping them for what He had called them to do. As a servant leader, you, too, must equip those you invite to serve with you. Let's look at the next step of how to equip others.

The second step to E.Q.U.I.P. others is to Qualify them for service.

Qualify in this session has two meanings. The first meaning is to meet certain expectations related to being a follower of Christ. These include the person's spiritual condition and a willingness to be a servant to others. The second meaning of qualify in this session is to know whether or not a person is competent for the ministry you have encouraged him or her to enter. This meaning relates to the person's S.E.R.V.E. profile (Week 3, Day 5, see p. 84) and specific skills related to the ministry he or she has agreed to do.

   1. A servant leader qualifies those he equips by holding them up to standards of discipleship, and by testing their willingness to be a servant to others.

   Jesus qualified those who followed Him by holding up high standards of discipleship. Let's return to *Luke 14*. It is the same chapter where we find the incident about the people wanting places at the head table. After Jesus' story about taking the back seats, Luke states, *"large crowds were traveling with Jesus" (Luke 14:25)*. Most church leaders would see this as a good thing, and would brag about it! Jesus, on the other hand, knew most of those following had no clue about what following Him actually meant.

   Read *Luke 14:26-27*. What are the qualifications of following Jesus?

Read *Luke 14:28-32*. What two examples did Jesus give to help the crowds consider what it would cost to follow Him?

Read *Luke 14:33*. What was Jesus' final qualification for being one of His disciples?

Jesus was very clear about the cost of discipleship. He risked losing large numbers in order to keep those who trusted Him and His mission. Jesus began equipping those who followed Him by holding up high standards of discipleship. As a leader who follows Jesus' example, you should make the cost of service to others very clear.

Important Note: No one is perfect. You can expect too much of a person before he is more mature in Christ. The danger of legalism exists any time you hold a person up to biblical standards for discipleship. No one lives up to the biblical ideal. You are a minister *"not of the letter but of the Spirit; for the letter kills, but the Spirit gives life" (2 Cor. 3:6)*. The opposite danger of legalism, however, is to have no standards for those who serve in the church. Too many churches suffer because those recruited to serve are not biblically qualified to serve. Seek a loving balance between biblical standards and the reality of human sinfulness.

Complete the following statement: The first meaning of to *qualify* is

2. *A servant leader qualifies those he equips by knowing their skills and giftedness related to the ministry he has asked them to do.*

The leader must know whether or not a person is competent for a particular ministry. A leader must ask the question, "Does this person know how to do what I am asking him to do?" The Bible provides a model for qualifying others for service in this sense.

Read *2 Timothy 2:2*. What did Paul tell Timothy to do?

The pattern of sharing the message of Jesus as outlined by Paul was:

Paul ⟶ Timothy ⟶ reliable men ⟶ others

Paul was Timothy's mentor. (You will learn about being and having a mentor in Week 5.) Paul trained Timothy as they traveled together *(Acts 16:1-5)*. When Paul felt Timothy was qualified to do ministry without him, he left Timothy in Ephesus to lead the church *(1 Tim. 1:3)*. Paul later wrote Timothy and told him to entrust what he learned from him to faithful men who would also *"be qualified to teach others" (2 Tim. 2:2)*.

> As a leader who follows Jesus' example, you should make the cost of service to others very clear.

Qualified in this verse means to be fit or competent for something. Paul told Timothy to find "reliable" or faithful men whom he could train to teach others. That pattern is still valid for equipping leaders today. A contemporary model of Paul's instructions would be:

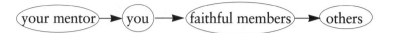

A Short Review

Complete the following statements as a review of today's study:
The second step to E.Q.U.I.P. others is

A servant leader qualifies those he equips by

Another way a servant leader qualifies those he equips is by

Personal Evaluation

Yesterday you prayerfully considered one or two people you could encourage to be involved in ministry, see page 89. Today, consider their qualifications to serve. Answer the following questions:

Do you know that they are growing disciples of Christ?
Name _____ ❏ Yes ❏ No   Name _____ ❏ Yes ❏ No

Do you know that they are reliable and faithful people?
Name _____ ❏ Yes ❏ No   Name _____ ❏ Yes ❏ No

Do you know their S.E.R.V.E. profiles?
Name _____ ❏ Yes ❏ No   Name _____ ❏ Yes ❏ No

If your answer is "Yes" to the last question, what does their S.E.R.V.E. profile tell you?

If your answer is "No," consider a time to help them through this study.

What skills would they need to learn before they would be qualified to do what you asked them to do?

One goal of servant leadership is to equip others for ministry. One aspect of equipping others is qualifying them to serve. Jesus refused to let anyone follow Him without telling them the qualifications of discipleship. How can the church do anything less?

Summary

- The second step to E.Q.U.I.P. others is to qualify them to serve.
- A servant leader qualifies those he equips by holding them up to biblical standards of discipleship and by testing their willingness to be a servant.
- Seek a loving balance between biblical standards and the reality of human sinfulness when holding others up to standards of holy living.
- A servant leader qualifies those he equips by knowing their skills related to the ministry in which they have agreed to serve.
- One way to qualify a person is to know his or her S.E.R.V.E. profile.

Again, here is this week's memory verse. As you complete today's work, read these words again, and then take a few moments to listen as God speaks.

"It was he who gave some to be apostles, some to be prophets, some to be evangelists, and some to be pastors and teachers, to prepare God's people for works of service, so that the body of Christ may be built up" (Eph. 4:11-12).

Now try covering the verse and writing it from memory in the space on this page. Don't worry if you can't yet write it word for word. By the end of the week, God will plant the words firmly in your heart, and its meaning will grow.

UNDERSTAND THEIR NEEDS

Today You Will:
- Learn the third step to E.Q.U.I.P. others.
- Observe how Jesus understood the needs of His disciples.
- Learn two ways to understand the needs of those you equip.
- Evaluate your progress in equipping another person for ministry.

Looking Back
Fill in the blanks with the phrases each letter represents in the process of equipping others.

     E _____ *(1 Thess. 5:11)*
     Q _____ *(2 Tim. 2:2)*

As a servant leader, you will encourage others to join you in ministry. You also will help qualify them for the service you have invited them to do. Today you will learn the next step in equipping others for ministry.

The Third Step To E.Q.U.I.P. Others
Summer is our family's athlete. She also happens to be my youngest daughter. Summer plays basketball and is a "flyer" on her all-star cheerleading team. (That's the one the team holds over their heads.) She also likes to play golf with me. Sometimes we will go to the driving range together. I will show Summer how to swing her club. I will then let her hit a ball. After her swing, I will tell her what to correct and praise her on what she did right! What I am doing with Summer is simply observing her and then helping her get better. She will never get a college scholarship for golf like her cousin while I am her coach, but she can get better if she allows another coach to equip her to play great golf.

The third step to E.Q.U.I.P. others is to Understand their needs and respond to them.

Jesus equipped His disciples by understanding their needs. Here's one example of how He did this.

Read *Matthew 17:14-21*.[1] This encounter came after Jesus' transfiguration. Jesus and His three closest followers came upon a crowd of people. A man came to Jesus in the crowd. What did he ask Jesus? *(Matt. 17:15)*

What did the man say about Jesus' disciples? *(Matt. 17:16)*

Later, the disciples who tried to heal the boy asked Jesus why they were unable to drive out the demon. What was Jesus' reply? *(Matt. 17:20-21; compare with Mark 9:29.)*

Jesus knew why His disciples were unable to heal the boy. He said they lacked faith and prayer in their lives. By observing the fruit of the disciples' ministry, Jesus understood their need to trust and pray more. They could not heal the boy, He said, because of their lack of faith and prayer. Jesus equipped His disciples by observing and understanding their needs.

How does this apply to your role as someone who equips others for ministry? Jesus observed His disciples as they followed Him. One way to understand the needs of those you equip is to observe them involved in ministry. Observation allows you to see what is needed for them to become more effective servants.

Place a check in the box by the statement(s) which you believe to be the best way to observe someone and understand his or her need.

❏ Wait for the one you are equipping to come to you and ask for help.
❏ Wait for someone to complain about how the one you recruited is doing his or her job.
❏ Spend time with him while he carries out his ministry.
❏ Ask others how the person is doing in his ministry.

One way to understand a person's need is to observe him as he does ministry. To equip someone means spending time with him in ministry so you can observe and understand his needs.

Another way to understand the needs of those you equip is to listen. Like my daughter who needed help with her golf swing, those you equip sometimes ask you for help with a need. Be certain to take the time to listen and respond.

Read *Luke 11:1-4*. What need did a disciple ask Jesus to address in his life?

How did Jesus respond?

The disciples watched Jesus perform many powerful acts among the people. They also watched Jesus spend many hours in prayer. They sensed a need for spiritual power in their own lives. They wanted what they observed in their Master's life. Once, as Jesus returned from a time of prayer, one of His disciples asked Him to teach them to pray. He responded to their need by teaching them to pray.

Jesus understood His follower's need because He listened to his request.

> *Jesus equipped His disciples by observing and understanding their needs.*

He equipped the twelve for ministry by modeling prayer in front of them and responding to their request when they asked Him about this habit in His life.

A second way to understand the needs of those you equip is to listen to their requests.

Record below some of the most frequently asked questions by those you are equipping. If you are not currently equipping someone, what questions do you think people may ask you?

    1.

    2.

    3.

You can understand needs simply by listening to the questions asked by those you recruit to serve.

Let's Review

Complete the following phrases to review today's lesson:

1. The third step to E.Q.U.I.P. others is to

2. One way to understand needs is

3. Another way to understand the needs of those you equip is

God has given you an opportunity to help build up the church by equipping others for works of service. This week, be in prayer each day about who you would invite to join you in ministry.

Summary

- The third step to E.Q.U.I.P. others is to understand their needs.
- To equip others is to spend time with them in ministry so you can observe and understand their needs.
- One way to understand a person's need is to observe that person as he or she does ministry.
- Another way to understand the needs of those you equip is to listen.
- By this time, you should have someone in mind whom you could invite to join you in ministry.

[1]Some translations do not include *verse 21*. Check your margins or study notes for text and explanation.

Again, here is this week's memory verse, this time with a few of the words omitted. Complete the verse. If you need a little help, don't worry. Simply turn back to page 85.

"It was he who gave some to be _____, some to be prophets, some to be evangelists, and some to be _____ and _____, to prepare God's people for works of service, so that the body of Christ may be built up" (_____ 4:11-12).

INSTRUCT THEM

Today You Will:
- Learn the fourth step to E.Q.U.I.P. others.
- Observe how Jesus instructed His followers.
- See how Paul instructed young Timothy in ministry.
- Evaluate possible areas of instruction as you equip others.

Looking Back:
Fill in the blanks with the phrases each letter represents.

E _____ *(1 Thess. 5:11)*

Q _____ *(2 Tim. 2:2)*

U _____ *(Luke 11:1)*

The Fourth Step To E.Q.U.I.P. Others

Leaders make a big mistake when they forget to instruct those they recruit. Too many times, leaders invite others to become involved in ministry and then leave them alone to guess what they should do. Problems always surface when workers go untrained.

The fourth step to E.Q.U.I.P. others is to Instruct them.

Instructing is part of leading. Followers need to know what is expected of them and how to do the task assigned to them. Jesus equipped His followers by instructing them. Let's look at His example.

Jesus' Example

Jesus constantly taught His disciples. He trained them about the nature of the kingdom of God *(Matt. 13)*. He explained His mission *(Mark 10:32-34)*. He performed a miracle to teach a lesson *(Mark 4:35-41)*. Occasionally, He had to instruct His disciples on their attitude about being His followers.

Read *Luke 17:7-10*. Jesus told a story to teach His followers an attitude of discipleship. Summarize the story Jesus told His disciples.

What was Jesus' point in this lesson?

Return to Jesus' teachings about being great and being first *(Mark 10:35-45, Week 1, Day 2, see p. 14)*. How does this story complement Jesus' instruction to His disciples about being great in the kingdom of God?

> *Followers need to know what is expected of them and how to do the task assigned to them.*

Jesus instructed His disciples to have the attitude of a servant. He taught that servants don't get special treatment when they do what is expected of them. This supported His earlier message about being great *(Mark 10:44-45)* and humbling yourself *(Luke 14:11)*. This instruction also came before His act of washing the disciples' feet *(John 13)*. Jesus equipped His disciples by teaching them in a variety of ways and settings to have a servant's heart.

Servant leaders equip those who follow them by instructing them in a variety of ways on different occasions.

Paul Instructed Timothy

Paul, the leader who built a worldwide web of churches, also instructed those he recruited for ministry. The clearest example of this practice comes from his letters to Timothy.

Timothy joined Paul on his second missionary journey *(Acts 16:1-3)*. Paul left him in Ephesus to lead the church there. Later, Paul wrote to Timothy and explained to him how he wanted the young leader to serve those given to his care.

Read *1 Timothy 4:11-16*. List Paul's instructions to Timothy.

v. 11

v. 12

v. 13

v. 14

v. 15

v. 16

> *Jesus instructed His disciples to have the attitude of a servant. He taught that servants don't get special treatment when they do what is expected of them.*

Paul instructed Timothy to teach the things he had outlined for him *(1 Tim. 4:11)*. He told the young man not to let others look down on him because he was young. Paul encouraged him to set an example in every area of his life for others to follow *(1 Tim. 4:12)*. Paul instructed the young pastor to devote himself to the public reading of Scripture, to preaching, and to teaching *(1 Tim. 4:13)*. Paul told him not to neglect his spiritual gift *(1 Tim. 4:14)*. Paul taught Timothy to be diligent in these matters so that others could see his progress *(1 Tim. 4:15)*. Finally, Paul instructed Timothy to watch his life and doctrine closely, because others depended on him *(1 Tim. 4:16)*.

Paul equipped Timothy by teaching him how to minister to those in his care. His instructions were clear and specific. Timothy did not have to wonder what his mentor expected of him. These instructions came out of Paul's experience and wisdom.

Servant leaders equip others by instructing them in the specifics of their ministry.

How Can You Instruct Others?

Let's assume for a moment you have found your place of servant leadership with the Sunday morning "Welcome Team." Your team's task is to make sure no new student is left to sit or be by herself. Your team of four people must know who is new and be friendly to those who are coming to your group for the first time. You have recruited your friend Steve to join you in this important ministry to guests. He has agreed to serve with you, but made it clear he knows nothing about a welcome ministry other than how to open a door, smile, and say, "Good Morning!" Steve looks to you for instruction. Answer the following questions:

What would you instruct Steve about his attitude as a welcome team member?

What would you say to Steve about the importance of his ministry?

What are some of the specifics of this ministry you could teach him?

What are some resources that would help him become an effective greeter?

While you may not be in a ministry of greeting new students, you can see how important instructions are to those you may recruit to help you. Servant leaders patiently instruct those they encourage to do ministry.

Summary

- The fourth step to E.Q.U.I.P. others is to instruct them.
- Jesus instructed His followers in several ways and on different occasions about their attitudes as servant leaders.
- Servant leaders equip those who follow them by instructing them in a variety of ways on a variety of occasions.
- Paul taught Timothy the specifics of how he wanted the young pastor to minister in Ephesus. Servant leaders equip others by instructing them in the specifics of their ministry.

Again, here is this week's memory verse, this time with a few more of the words omitted. Try completing the verse without looking back.

"It was he who gave some to be _____, some to be prophets, some to be _____, and some to be _____ and _____, to prepare God's people for _____ of _____, so that the body of Christ may be built up" (_____).

Take a few moments now to write a few statements above concerning what God has said to you this week through this verse, and how His words have become more meaningful in your life.

PRAY FOR THEM

Today You Will:
- Learn the fifth step to E.Q.U.I.P. others.
- Observe how Jesus prayed for those He called to serve.
- See how Paul asked for prayer from those he appointed for service.
- Conclude your checklist to equip another person for ministry.

Looking Back:
Fill in the blanks with the phrases each letter represents.

E _____ *(1 Thess. 5:11)*
Q _____ *(2 Tim. 2:2)*
U _____ *(Luke 11:1)*
I _____ *(1 Tim. 4:11)*

> *The final and most important step to E.Q.U.I.P. others for ministry is to pray for them.*

Up to this point, each of these actions can be done in human strength. You can encourage others under your own power. Your motivation to involve others can simply be because you need help! You can qualify others by your own efforts and standards. You can understand the needs of those you recruit by watching and listening to them. You can even instruct them in attitudes and specifics of their ministry based upon human decision. But one thing would be lacking: the power of God in their lives. Jesus observed a lack of power in His disciples when they could not cast out a demon *(Matt. 17:19-21)*. Something was missing. This is why the final and most important step to E.Q.U.I.P. others for ministry is to pray for them.

The Fifth Step To E.Q.U.I.P. Others
We have seen how Jesus modeled every step of equipping others for ministry. Jesus made this final step a priority in His ministry. In His final hours with those He loved, He prayed for them. Let's look at this special prayer.
  Read *John 17:6-19*. Jesus prayed for His disciples' ministry.
- Jesus knew He had taught them what they needed to know about His mission and God. " '*I gave them the words you gave me*' " *(John 17:8)*.
- He prayed that they remain one in spirit and purpose. " '*Protect them by the power of your name . . . so that they may be one as we are one*' " *(John 17:11)*.
- He prayed that they would have joy in their ministry. " '*I say these things while I am still in the world, so that they may have the full measure of my joy within them*' " *(John 17:13)*.

- Jesus asked the Father to protect them from the evil one. " *'My prayer is not that you take them out of the world but that you protect them from the evil one'* " *(John 17:15)*.
- He prayed that they be made holy by the truth of God's word. " *'Sanctify them by the truth; your word is truth'* " *(John 17:17)*.

Jesus equipped His disciples by praying for them.

The fifth step to E.Q.U.I.P. others is to Pray for them.

Paul, too, prayed regularly for those he set aside for ministry. (For examples, read *Phil. 1:3-6* and *Eph. 3:14-19*.) Paul knew the power of prayer for all the saints as well as for himself.

Read *Ephesians 6:18-20*. What was Paul's conclusion to his teaching about spiritual conflict? *(Eph. 6:18)*

The verses prior to these are more familiar to most Christians. *Verse 18,* however, is the conclusion to Paul's teaching about how God protects those who follow Jesus. Paul taught that prayer is our most powerful weapon. He asked the church to pray for all the saints on all occasions. He also asked for prayer for himself.

Read again *Ephesians 6:19-20*. What did Paul request in these verses?

Paul knew the power of prayer. He asked that the Christians in Ephesus pray for him while he ministered. He did not ask that he be released from prison. (This would be what most of us would ask.) He asked that he be given the words to witness boldly for Christ! He asked that he receive the power and courage to speak fearlessly concerning the mystery of the gospel. Paul not only prayed for others, he asked others to pray for him.

Servant leaders pray for those they equip for ministry. They also ask for prayers so that they may lead boldly. Here we see the unique nature of Christian leadership. Leaders in the church know that their power comes from God, not themselves. They also know that they are most effective when others support them in prayer. Church leaders are helpless without the prayers of others. These prayers may be all that keeps them standing in times of struggle and conflict.

After a long Wednesday coupled with a youth worship service that night Stacey was ready to make his twenty-minute drive home with a quick stop by McDonalds for his favorite value meal. In the process of shutting down "The Barn," Allison, one of our students, approached him and with a humble spirit and not seeking any favoritism, quietly said, "I just want you to know that I pray for you and your family every day." A sudden sense of peace surged through him and with a grateful response, he simply said, "Thank you." It wasn't a few weeks later that another student,

Leaders in the church know that their power comes from God, not themselves.

Angie, told him the same thing in a slightly different way. Stacey is fully aware that those prayers are sustainers to both his ministry and his family. Allison and Angie are true servants who daily lift up those who serve.

No servant leader should stand to lead until he kneels to pray with those he serves.

The power of equipping others is not in technique, but in prayer. Prayer should be a part of every step to equip others. Prayer gives discernment, protection, and power to those who lead. Prayer is God's answer to our weakness as leaders.

Summary

- The fifth step to E.Q.U.I.P. others is to pray for them.
- Jesus equipped His disciples by praying for them.
- Paul, too, prayed regularly for those he set aside for ministry.
- Servant leaders pray for those they equip for ministry. They also ask for prayer so that they may lead boldly.
- Prayer is God's answer to our weakness as leaders.

Let's Review

Complete the following phrases to review this week's lessons:

1. The first step to E.Q.U.I.P. others is to

2. The second step to E.Q.U.I.P. others is to

3. The third step to E.Q.U.I.P. others is to

4. The fourth step to E.Q.U.I.P. others is to

5. The fifth step to E.Q.U.I.P. others is to

Complete the chart below to help you determine where you are in the process to equip someone for ministry.

My E.Q.U.I.P. Progress

Name of person I can encourage: _____

The ministry I have in mind is: _____

He or she is qualified for this because: _____

His/her potential needs may be: _____

Potential areas of instruction may be: _____

I can pray for him or her in these ways: _____

This week introduced you to an important aspect of servant leadership: equipping others for service. Next week you will see the best way to multiply your effectiveness as a leader: through the power of team ministry.

THIS WEEK'S
MEMORY VERSE

"Calling the Twelve to him, he sent them out two by two and gave them authority over evil spirits"

(Mark 6:7, NIV).

For years Stacey ran Wednesday nights as a one-man show. A typical youth service found him setting up all by himself in the afternoon and greeting students minutes before 7:00 p.m. He would start with announcements, lead music, pray, have more music, a bible study and top it off with a closing prayer. Oh yeah, let's not forget he ran his own sound, too. As far as he knew that was his job. After all, he was the one who got a paycheck every two weeks. The problem was he was doing the entire ministry and never taking time to equip others to do the work of ministry.

When Stacey began serving as Youth Minister at Legacy Drive, he began with same "one man" approach. A month after he started, however, Greg came on board. He was a gifted communicator, and Stacey turned the majority of the speaking over to him. Greg brought a friend, Todd, a committed worship leader, and Stacey suddenly found himself just helping set up sound and making announcements. At first it was a test of the ego, but he soon realized that effective ministry wasn't contingent upon him doing everything. Within six months Todd left. Stacey then asked a student to lead worship along with other students in the youth group. Now our X-treme event on Wednesday evenings is primarily a student-run ministry with tech teams, welcome teams, and a set-up and breakdown team. Stacey admitted that he was both embarrassed and disappointed that he did everything and never took the time to build a team.

Servant leaders team with others to serve the mission of God. They know effective leadership is not a solo venture. Leadership is a team sport. Servant leaders also know that teams move the ball down the field to reach a goal. They know they are most effective when they can team with others who are equipped to meet a specific need.

Jesus' earthly ministry revolved around building a team of close followers. He called them, equipped them, and mobilized them into a team for ministry. After Jesus had completed His mission on earth, these disciples would complete the mission He called them to do. Jesus modeled team ministry for those He called to be servant leaders. He built a team so that the mission of making disciples would continue after he had physically left the scene.

This week is about team ministry. You will learn some basic principles about how teams work, and you will be encouraged to begin forming a ministry team as part of your role as a servant leader.

This week concludes your study of Jesus on Leadership. You will want to take time to look beyond this study to where Christ wants you to serve. This study is not the end of your understanding of servant leadership. It is only the beginning.

This Week You Will:

- See that a servant leader leads best through ministry teams. (Day 1)
- Learn that teams work best when they work Together. (Day 1)
- Examine how leaders Empower those on their team. (Day 2)
- Observe the biblical principle of Accountability. (Day 3)
- Learn that the best leaders are Mentors to those on their team. (Day 4)
- Learn the four next steps to becoming a servant leader, and make decisions about what you will do to continue the process of becoming a servant leader.(Day 5)

TOGETHERNESS

Today You Will:
- Understand that leadership is a team sport.
- Define *team ministry*.
- Learn your role as a team leader.
- Observe how Jesus modeled team ministry with His disciples.
- Learn the characteristics of working together as a team.
- Examine some signs of a team that is together.
- Evaluate your willingness to foster togetherness on a team.

> *A leader is more like a player on a soccer team than like a pro golfer on tour.*

Leadership is not a solo venture. It is a team sport. A leader is more like a player on a soccer team than like a pro golfer on tour. Leaders are not lone rangers. They involve others to reach a shared goal. Team leaders are player coaches. You will never be an effective leader until you include those you lead in what you do. Leaders fail when they believe their efforts alone will achieve a group's goal.

Look back at the introduction to Week 1, page 6. Write the stated purpose of this study:

The purpose of this study is that you become a servant leader in team ministry. Servant leaders serve best when they serve with others. While needs do arise that demand the help of only one person, usually two or more persons meet needs more effectively. You will serve best as a leader when you team with others. Let's take a look at team ministry.

Jesus On Team Ministry

Jesus taught and modeled servant leadership (Week 1). He equipped His disciples for ministry (Week 4). Jesus also modeled team ministry. He seldom did ministry by Himself. Jesus was Master, and needed no one else to help meet needs. Yet no matter what He was doing, He ministered with His disciples nearby. He usually had at least three disciples with Him wherever He went. By constantly having His closest followers near Him, He showed how the best lessons came from the classroom of experience. Jesus did not need a ministry team, but He built one so that ministry would continue when He returned to the Father.

Matthew, Mark, and Luke tell how Jesus commissioned His followers to do ministry in His name. *Matthew 10* is a disciple's manual for ministry. Mark recorded the fact that Jesus sent His disciples out two by two *(Mark 6:7)*. He knew the advantage of two serving together as a team rather than one trying to meet needs alone.

Jesus modeled team ministry. His disciples followed that example. When the Holy Spirit directed the church in Antioch to send members out to share the gospel with the Gentiles, God's Spirit told the church to select two members. After prayer and fasting, the church sent them out *(Acts 13:1-3)*. Ministry teams are how the early church met the need of evangelism. Ministry teams are how the church of the twenty-first century will continue to meet needs effectively.

WHY T.E.A.M.?

A team is a group of people bound together by a commitment to reach a shared goal related to the mission. A team can be a group of college students playing intramural football. It can be a group of researchers seeking the cure for a disease. A group of Sunday School workers teaching the Bible to a room full of four-year-olds also can be a team. A team can put a space probe on Mars or feed the poor.

Churches have begun to see the advantages of teams. Richard Ross, a youth ministry consultant, LifeWay Christian Resources, has introduced the concept of Lead Teams in the church where he serves. A Lead Team is a group of youth workers, parents of youth and teenagers that takes "ultimate responsibility for an event. The youth minister helps teams who are fully committed to seeing events through. The Lead Team concept changes the place where the buck stops."[1] So how do teams apply to servant leadership and your ministry?

You have spent four weeks studying servant leadership and the importance of meeting needs. Servant leadership begins when a disciple takes the role of a servant to meet a need. Servant leadership is also about setting self aside so Christ can be Lord. Write your own definition of servant leadership in the space below:

Team ministry affords servant leaders a way to multiply their callings to meet the needs of others. My definition is "Team ministry is a group of disciples bound together under the lordship of Christ who are committed to the shared goal of meeting a particular need related to the mission." Team ministry is how servant leaders generally do the work of ministry. This week you will discover four characteristics of team ministry: Togetherness, Empowerment, Accountability, and Mentoring.

Team Ministry Begins When You Are Together With Others

Team ministry occurs where there is a sense of being part of a team. The first characteristic of a team is the sense that, "We are in this together." Team members sense that each person belongs, and that each is respected by the other team members. Team ministry starts when those on the team sense they are together for a reason greater than themselves.

> Ministry teams are how the early church met the need of evangelism. Ministry teams are how the church of the twenty-first century will continue to meet needs effectively.

Teams form to reach a common goal. Like the X-treme teams mentioned in this week's introduction, teams have a reason to form and function. Evangelism teams form to reach the goal of introducing others to Christ. Worship teams form to lead churches to worship God more effectively. Lead teams plan and execute events. Teams have a purpose for forming. That purpose drives them throughout their existence. When they have reached their goal, the team disbands or re-directs its energy to other goals. The team celebrates its performance, and its members may or may not re-form into a new team.

Unity is a key to success. Read *Matthew 12:30*. What were two options related to being on Jesus' team?

Jesus insisted that those who follow Him share His same values and purposes. The disciples either agreed with who He was and what He did, or they worked against Him. Jesus even scolded Peter for not supporting the Master's clear purpose for ministry *(Matt. 16:23)*.

Team members have a deep sense that they share a common and important reason for being together. This gives the team a sense of togetherness. This sense of unity and purpose is the glue that holds the team together until it has reached its goal. Division in a team can be deadly to its existence.

When Teams Are Together

We have already noted that the first characteristic of an effective team is a sense that, "We are in this together." What are some signs that a team is together? Write your ideas in the margin.

We have seen how Jesus insisted that unity be part of His ministry team of disciples. Another sign of togetherness is that He shared authority and responsibility with those on His team. As the team's leader, Jesus modeled shared leadership. He invited His followers to do what He did with His same power and authority. This instilled confidence among His followers.

Read *Mark 6:6-13*. What two actions did Jesus take when He sent out His disciples as ministry teams? *(Mark 6:7)*

What other instructions did Jesus give His followers? *(Mark 6:8-11)*

What were the results of the twelve's mission? *(Mark 6:12-13)*

When Jesus sent out His twelve closest followers, He sent them out in teams of two. Jesus knew the proverb, *"Two are better than one, because they have a good return for their work: If one falls down, his friend can help him up. But pity the man who falls and has no one to help him up! Also, if two lie down together, they will keep warm. But how can one keep warm alone? Though one may be overpowered, two can defend themselves. A cord of three strands is not quickly broken" (Eccl. 4:9-12).*

Jesus shared with the disciples His authority over the evil ones they would encounter *(Mark 6:7)*. Jesus instructed them to take nothing except a staff for their journey *(Mark 6:8)*. They were to take no extra clothing *(Mark 6:9)*. They were to stay in the same home in each town they entered *(Mark 6:10)*. If someone did not welcome them, they were to shake the dust off their feet as a sign of their displeasure *(Mark 6:11)*. The teams of two went out and preached the gospel *(Mark 6:12)*. They experienced success *(Mark 6:13)*. Jesus shared His leadership with the teams by sending and empowering them to do what He commissioned them to do.

Servant leaders in team ministry must keep a balance between doing things themselves and encouraging others to participate. Although he or she may appear to have a servant attitude, a person who does the team's work alone is not a genuine servant leader. Richard Ross explains how Youth Ministers are not effective when he or she does the work of ministry alone:

> Most youth ministers have learned to delegate certain tasks while preparing for an activity. That is the only way they have survived so far. The challenge comes when preparation for several activities is underway simultaneously. Every subcommittee or group of helpers feels responsible to the youth minister. That means they all turn to the same staff member with every question or problem…And, because those delegated to are merely 'helpers,' they may be tempted to let a responsibility slide if they get busy.[2]

Jesus fostered a sense of togetherness by sending out His disciples in twos rather than alone. He also shared leadership with His disciples. This, too, gave them a sense of being part of His team to spread the gospel.

Personal Evaluation

1. Today, begin praying about persons who you can lead to become a ministry or lead team. These may be persons you will equip for servanthood, persons who share your same enthusiasm for ministry. Begin building your potential team members by making a list of those who share your passion for a certain ministry need or event. (You may want to refer back to Week 3, Day 5, see p. 83.) Write the names of those who come to mind in the margin.

2. Consider your feelings about team ministry. What could you do for the kingdom if you had six or eight other disciples who shared your heart for ministry? Write your ideas in the margin.

Jesus fostered a sense of togetherness.

Team ministry is about Christian servants committed to meeting needs related to our mission to make disciples. Jesus and His disciples have modeled it for us. And you can model this for the rest of the church. Prayerfully consider how God can use you in team ministry.

Summary

- The goal of this study is that you become a servant leader in team ministry.
- Team ministry involves a group of disciples bound together under the lordship of Christ, committed to the shared goal of meeting the needs of others related to the mission.
- Jesus sent out His followers to do ministry in teams rather than one by one.
- As a servant leader, you are willing to share leadership with those who team with you to do ministry.
- The first characteristic of a team is, "We are in this together." Unity is a key to effectiveness.
- As His team's leader, Jesus modeled shared leadership. He invited His followers to do what He did with the same power and authority.
- A team is together when its leader shares leadership and authority with those on the team.
- Servant leaders in team ministry must keep a balance between doing things themselves and encouraging others to participate.

[1]Richard Ross, Youth Ministry Update (March, 1994).
[2]Ibid.

Again, here is this week's memory verse. As you complete today's work, read these words of Jesus aloud a few times. Spend a few more moments alone with God, and listen to Him speak to your heart concerning servant leadership.

"Calling the Twelve to him, he sent them out two by two and gave them authority over evil spirits" (Mark 6:7).

day 2

EMPOWERMENT

Today You Will:

- Learn how effective team leaders empower those on the team.
- Observe how Jesus empowered His disciples.
- See how Paul empowered Aquila and Priscilla.
- Review how you can empower others in team ministry.

Write the seventh principle of servant leadership in the margin (Week 1, Day 4, see p. 25.)

Servant leaders in team ministry empower those on their team to reach a shared goal related to the mission. Members of a team must feel they are a part of the team and empowered by their leader, or the team will not do its best work. If team members are not empowered, the leader does all the work—and that is not a team. Richard Ross described the role of the youth minister in empowering Lead Team chairpersons when he wrote:

> "Every Lead Team chairperson needs to feel the full support of the youth minister. Every chairperson needs:
> - Quick access to the youth minister;
> - Feedback that the youth minister is knowledgeable about the team's general plans;
> - Assurance that the youth minister is ready and willing to accept appropriate assignments from the team.
> - Continuing expressions of confidence, enthusiasm, and encouragement from the youth minister."[1]

Ross reminds the youth minister, the leader, that his or her responsibility is to make sure the chairpersons of the various Lead Teams have all they need to accomplish their assigned goal. Empowerment is about giving team members authority and resources enough to do their part of the work.

Every Member Is Important

Team ministry means that every member has a place on the team. Each one can make a contribution toward the group's goal. Different spiritual gifts, experiences, relational styles, vocational skills, and enthusiasm make a ministry team complete. Teams demand different skills and gifts. Peter Drucker, an authority on business management has noted:

> "A common mistake is to believe that because individuals are all on the same team, they all think alike and act alike. Not so. The purpose of a team is to make the strengths of each person effective, and his or her weaknesses irrelevant."[2]

> *If team members are not empowered, the leader does all the work.*

Putting a team together means finding persons who share a common goal with you but who may be different from how you think or act. Team ministry reinforces the biblical teaching of the church having many parts but one body.

Return to Week 2, Day 2 (see p. 37). Paul addressed two harmful thoughts that could destroy the church. You can find them in *1 Corinthians 12:14-26*. Write those two harmful thoughts below.

(see p. 37)

Paul warns each member of the church against two extremely harmful attitudes: (1) the feeling that I don't belong and have nothing to contribute to the church; and (2) that I could become totally self-sufficient and not need the other members of the body of Christ. The Bible teaches that every member belongs, and every part needs all the others. Team ministry affirms this biblical principle. Every member has a place of service in the church. Servant leaders who build ministry teams will help every member to find a place of service. Thus, "I don't belong" and "I don't need you" are thoughts that undermine the unity of the body.

Jesus Empowered His Disciples

The mission of every New Testament church is to make disciples. You don't have to put a task force together to discover this. Jesus co-missioned with the twelve to make disciples: to turn lost, secular people into maturing disciples of Christ. Every church should be about this mission given to it by Christ. But how were the disciples then and disciples now to find the power to do this mission?

Read *Matthew 28:18-20*. What did Jesus say to His disciples before He ascended into heaven?

Jesus stated that all authority had been given to Him. Based on this truth, He sent out His followers to make disciples. Jesus empowered His disciples by sharing His authority with them. You saw how Moses empowered his leaders with authority to make decisions among the people of Israel (*Ex. 18;* Week 1, Day 4, see pages 24 and 25). Yesterday, you saw how Jesus sent His disciples out two by two and gave them His authority over the evil ones they would encounter *(Mark 6:7)*.

Read *Acts 1:8*. What did Jesus tell the disciples they would receive, and what would they become as a result?

Jesus promised His followers that they would receive power to do their mission " *'when the Holy Spirit comes on you.' "* They would then become witnesses to that power in their lives as they sought to carry out the Great Commission. Jesus empowered His disciples to become witnesses by giving

> "I don't belong" and "I don't need you" are thoughts that undermine the unity of the body.

them the power of His presence, the Holy Spirit. He gave His missions team the power they needed to reach the goal of world evangelism. Jesus empowered His disciples to reach the goal by giving them the authority of His name and the power of His presence. With these resources, the disciples were able to make the right decisions and act with authority to carry out God's plan.

What two things did Jesus give His disciples to empower them to carry out His mission?

As a servant leader in team ministry, what two things must you give your team members in order for them to reach the goals you agree upon together?

Paul Empowered His Workers

You do not empower people with a memo. Empowerment does not happen with the stroke of a pen or keyboard. You empower people in real time. It takes time and effort to empower someone to do the work of a team member. Paul did this with many on his ministry team by living with them and giving them responsibilities of service.

Read *Acts 18:1-4.* Who did Paul meet and begin ministering with when he came to Corinth? *(Acts 18:2)*

What vocational skill did they share in common? *(Acts 18:3)*

What did Paul do with Aquila and Priscilla? *(Acts 18:3)*

Paul met a couple from Rome when he came to Corinth. Like himself, they were tentmakers. Luke tells us that Paul *"stayed and worked with them" (verse 3).* While on mission, Paul joined this Christian couple to reach the goal of telling all people about Christ.[3]

Read *Acts 18:18.* Who was with Paul as he traveled to his next missions point?

Paul stayed in Corinth for a year and six months *(Acts 18:11).* What do you think happened during this time which made Aquila and Priscilla want to travel with him?

> *You do not empower people with a memo.*

A year and a half after his arrival in Corinth, Paul moved on in his journey of world evangelism. Luke tells us that Priscilla and Aquila were part of Paul's ministry team when he left Corinth. We do not know what happened to make them want to go, but Paul possibly recruited and trained them to do the work of missions. They also may have wanted to support Paul with their tentmaking so he could minister full time. Team ministry means all members contribute to the goal in their own ways.

Read *Acts 18:19-21.* What does Paul do with Priscilla and Aquila?

Why do you think he did this?

When Paul arrived in Ephesus, he realized the need for mature believers who could help the growing church there. He left Priscilla and Aquila in Ephesus to help lead the church. Paul equipped and empowered his two friends to become servant leaders. He left them in Ephesus because he knew they were trained to do the ministry they had been called to do. They were servant leaders who desired to meet a need in the Ephesian church. This is also evidenced by their response to Apollos when he arrived in Ephesus *(Acts 18:24-26).* They felt free to address a need in the young teacher's ministry. (We will see this again as we look at mentoring on Day 4 of this week's study.)

How did Paul empower Priscilla and Aquila?
1. He taught and modeled the gospel as he lived and worked with them. They apparently became part of his ministry team in Corinth.
2. He invited them to join his ministry team as it traveled to the next missions point.
3. He left them in Ephesus to create their own ministry team as he continued his journey.

To follow Paul's pattern of empowerment, you must . . .
1. Teach and model the gospel as you live and work with other believers.
2. Invite others to join you on your ministry team when you see they can contribute to the goal of your mission.
3. Empower them to take on ministry by themselves and form their own ministry teams.

Jesus modeled the *what* of empowerment. You empower your team with the authority of your position and the power of your presence to reach your goal.

Paul modeled the *how* of empowerment. You empower your team by living and working with them and inviting them to take on more responsibility along the way.

Personal Evaluation

1. List some ways that you can empower your team members by sharing with them the resources of authority and power.

What authority do you have to share with them?

How can you share "the power of your presence" with them to aid them in their work? What are some ways you can spend time with them to help them understand and do the work of the team?

2. What are some ways you can empower your team members like Paul empowered Aquila and Priscilla?

How can you "live and work" with them?

Close today's study by claiming God's authority and power in your life and praying for the wisdom to empower those who are part of your ministry team.

Summary

- Team ministry means that every member has a place on the team, and each one can make a contribution toward the goal.
- Servant leaders in team ministry empower those on their team to reach a shared goal.
- Empowerment is about giving team members authority and resources enough to do their part of the work.
- Jesus modeled the "what" of empowerment. You empower your team with the authority of your position and the power of your presence to reach their goal.
- Paul modeled the "how" of empowerment. You empower your team by living and working with them and inviting them to take on more responsibility along the way.

[1]Richard Ross, Youth Ministry Update, (June, 1995).
[2]Peter F. Drucker, *Managing the Nonprofit Organization* (New York: HarperCollins Publishers, Inc., 1990), 152-53.
[3]Scholars argue whether Aquila and Priscilla were believers before or after they met Paul. What is important is that we do know by *Acts 18:18* they are followers of Christ and co-workers with Paul.

Again, here is this week's memory verse. As you complete today's work, read these words again, and then take a few moments to listen as God speaks.

"Calling the Twelve to him, he sent them out two by two and gave them authority over evil spirits" *(Mark 6:7).*

Now try covering the verse and writing it from memory in the space here. Don't worry if you can't yet write it word for word. By the end of the week, God will plant the words firmly in your heart, and its meaning will grow.

ACCOUNTABILITY

Today You Will:

- Examine the biblical principle of accountability.
- Learn how effective team leaders are accountable for those on the team.
- Observe how Jesus held His disciples accountable to His goals.
- See the importance of accountability among team members.

Accountability makes team ministry possible. It is the ability to account for who you are and what you have done. It is the glue that keeps team members together and working toward the same goal. With it, team members can count on others to do what they say they will do. Without it, members decide on their own when, how, and if they will do their part of the work. Trust of others on the team and commitment to the same goal are elements of accountability in team ministry.

Before we apply this truth more directly to team ministry, let's see what Jesus taught about accountability.

Jesus On Accountability

Jesus taught that everyone will give an account to a holy God for their words and deeds. Jesus said this when He addressed a group of religious leaders who accused Him of working for Satan. He said, " *'But I tell you that men will have to give account on the day of judgment for every careless word they have spoken'* " (Matt. 12:36).

Paul reminded the Roman Christians that, *"Each of us will give an account of himself to God"* (Rom. 14:12). Peter encouraged his readers not to worry if pagans did not understand their lifestyle. They, too, *"will have to give account to him who is ready to judge the living and the dead"* (1 Pet. 4:5). Accountability to God means to give an account for your behavior while on earth. To give an account simply means to tell the truth to the person to whom you are responsible for what you have done and said.

If you had to give an account to God today for what you have done and said, would that be acceptable to God?

❏ Yes   ❏ No

Why did you respond in this way? Write your response in the margin.

The Bible teaches that accountability is part of your relationship with God. This sense of giving an account to God should affect how you live your life. You will find it hard to be accountable to people if you do not trust that you are accountable to God.

Mutual accountability is being responsible for what you say and do to persons you commit yourself to. An example of this is marriage. A married couple promises to be faithful to one another. They are then responsible to one another to carry out that promise. Accountability in marriage keeps the couple together because it builds trust and displays commitment.

List some promises you are responsible to others to keep. These may be friends or students in band or on a team with you.

1.

2.

3.

Teams work best when their members are accountable to one another. Accountability applies to every member of the team, including the leader.

Leaders are accountable to God for those in their care.

Leaders Are Accountable For Their Group

Read *Hebrews 13:17*, which is printed in the margin. Underline the reasons why the writer asked members of the church to obey their leaders.

The writer to the Hebrews insisted that members in the church obey their leaders. He gave two reasons for this command: (1) leaders are accountable for those in the church, and (2) their work will be a joy instead of a burden if the members follow. This verse teaches that leaders are accountable for those under their care. Servant leaders are accountable for persons on their team as they work together to reach their shared goal.

This verse also teaches that members should follow their leaders. Members are responsible to their leader to follow his or her guidance. Trust in the leader and commitment to the church's mission cement this relationship between church leader and follower. The result is a joyful leader. A joyful leader is an advantage for those on the team! If the leader is free to guide, then he is free to move the group in the direction of their shared goal.

"Obey your leaders and submit to their authority. They keep watch over you as men who must give an account. Obey them so that their work will be a joy, not a burden, for that would be of no advantage to you." (Heb. 13:17).

Leaders Are Accountable For The Goal

Servant leaders are accountable to keep the team focused on their goal. Jesus modeled this for those in the school of servant leadership as He taught His disciples the true nature of His mission.

Read *Mark 8:27-30*. What did Peter confess about who Jesus is?

Peter confessed that Jesus is the Messiah. He committed himself to Jesus' goal of carrying out God's plan of redemption.

Read *Mark 8:31-32*. How did Peter respond to Jesus' prediction?

Peter refused to accept Jesus' words about His suffering and death. He pulled Jesus aside and rebuked Him. Peter trusted his concept of the Christ rather than what Jesus had taught. Peter's ideas threatened the mission of the Messiah and the unity of the disciples.

Read *Mark 8:33*. How did Jesus respond to Peter's rebuke?

Churches function best when members accept the relational styles of others and seek to meet the needs of those persons, while never compromising the message of Christ.

Jesus knew the danger of Peter's attitude. The team of disciples had to be together on who Jesus was and the nature of His mission. Jesus confronted Peter's words by saying, " *'Get behind me, Satan!'* " Jesus called Peter "Satan" because the disciple offered the same easy path to victory, which Satan had posed to Jesus in the wilderness *(Luke 4:9-12)*. Jesus knew the Messiah must suffer and die to complete the Father's mission of redemption. Jesus was accountable to the Father to meet this goal. As a leader, He knew the need for His followers to stay committed to the same goal He was living to reach.

Accountability Among The Team Members

"No group ever becomes a team until it can hold itself accountable as a team."[1] No baseball team can get to the World Series until every team member makes himself accountable to the others to reach this goal. Team members make themselves responsible to one another to do their part in reaching the shared goal. When you make yourself responsible to others on a ministry team, you become accountable to them. Team ministry means making yourself accountable to the other team members to reach your shared goal.

Team accountability can start when each member has a servant leader's heart. Write below the third principle of servant leadership:

Jesus taught that greatness among His followers begins with being a servant to others. Being first starts with giving up personal rights to meet the needs of others *(Mark 10:44)*. Team accountability can happen when team members become "servants" to the goal of the team and "slaves" to those on the team to help them reach that goal. Leith Anderson, a pastor and author, reminds us:

> "It should surprise us that so much is said about leaders and so little about followers, especially among Christians committed to the Bible. The Bible says comparatively little about leadership and a great deal about followership. Jesus did not invite Peter, Andrew, James, and John to become leaders immediately. He said, 'Follow Me!' "[2]

Jesus called His disciples to follow Him. They became leaders only after Jesus trained them and empowered them with His Holy Spirit.

The second principle of servant leadership states that: "Servant leaders follow Jesus rather than seek a position." You have seen how Jesus gave up His position in heaven to bring salvation to the world. You observed how He led from a servant's position. Jesus is your example of a servant leader who gave up position to meet the needs of others. Servant leaders share leadership with others to reach a common goal.

Team accountability can happen when team members become servants to the goal of ministry and slaves to those on the team to help them reach that goal.

Servant leaders also know how to follow. Each person's first steps as a leader began as a follower. Disciples are learners who fall in line behind their Master. Since servant leaders know how to follow, they willingly allow others to lead when another S.E.R.V.E. profile fits the need better than their own. Servant leaders share leadership with others when the need dictates. This is an important aspect of accountability to God and to the team.

Personal Evaluation

Complete the following statements in the space provided:

1. The concept of accountability is hard for me to accept because . . .

2. I have experienced a sense of accountability to others when I . . .

3. If you are a ministry or Lead Team leader, write the goal to which you ask your team to be accountable.

4. List some ways you can build trust and commitment among your team members to help them become accountable to one another.

Summary

- Accountability makes team ministry possible.
- Trust of others on the team and commitment to the same goal are elements of accountability in team ministry.
- Jesus taught that every person will give an account to a holy God for his or her words and deeds.
- Mutual accountability is being responsible to those you commit yourself to for what you say and do.
- Servant leaders are accountable to keep the team focused on their goal.
- Team ministry means making yourself accountable to the other team members to reach your shared goal.

[1]Katzenbach and Smith, *The Wisdom of Teams* (Boston: Harvard Business School Press, 1993), 60.
[2]Leith Anderson, *A Church for the 21st Century* (Minneapolis: Bethany House, 1992), 222.

> Servant leaders share leadership with others when the need dictates. This is an important aspect of accountability to God and to the team.

Again, here is this week's memory verse, this time with a few of the words omitted. Complete the verse. If you need a little help, don't worry. Simply turn back to page 103.

"Calling the Twelve to him, he sent them out two by two and gave them _____ over evil spirits" (_____ 6:7).

day 4

MENTORING

Today You Will:

- Examine the practice of mentoring.
- Observe how Jesus mentored His disciples.
- See how Paul instructed Timothy to be a mentor.
- Consider your need for a mentor in your life.

> Mentors model what they want their followers to do. Their actions weigh as heavy as their words.

A mentor is a guide. Mentors lead others through new terrain because they have been there before and are equipped to lead. Mentors model what they want their followers to do. Their actions weigh as heavy as their words. Leaders in team ministry guide where the team is going and model the Christian lifestyle they want team members to follow.

In the Spring of 1998, we were gearing up to start a Sunday night discipleship course for students which would be offered during the summer months. Gina, one of our Youth Sunday School Staffers came to me with a guy named Tom. After meeting him and his wife over lunch I knew that God had given us the privilege of sitting under the teachings of a truly gifted man, who not only shares incredible biblical truths, but also has a tremendous heart for teenagers. What we didn't know about Tom at that point was that he also is a mentor. Once a millionaire, Tom now devotes his time to mentoring students, young adults and even some who are his peers. Tom mentors several individuals a week. He is a servant leader who seeks to invest in the lives of others that they too may one day mentor others.

To this day Tom is still leading our high school discipleship class "Unplugged" on Sunday nights and leads a Bible study called "Icthus" at his house every Tuesday night where approximately 60 teenagers cram into his living room to the hear the truths from God's word. Tom multiplies Christ in the lives of others through a ministry of mentoring.

Servant leaders are mentors to persons with them in team ministry. Mentoring is how the work of Christ is passed on to the next generation of servant leaders. To mentor is to multiply Christ in the life of another.

Fill in these blanks.

A mentor is a _____.

Team leaders _____ where the team is going and _____ the Christian lifestyle they want their members to follow.

Jesus On Mentoring

Jesus guided His disciples and modeled for them how they should live as His followers. When Jesus called His disciples to follow Him, He meant for them to follow His example as well as His feet! Read the following passages and record some ways Jesus mentored His disciples.

How Jesus Mentored His Disciples

Jesus mentored His disciples by teaching them. *Matthew 5, 6,* and *7* record Jesus' Sermon on the Mount, Jesus' teachings about how kingdom people live. Earlier in this study, you learned more about His teaching ministry as He taught His disciples concerning leadership *(Mark 10:35-45).*

Jesus also mentored His followers by demonstrating the power of God in their lives. When the disciples thought there was no way to feed a crowd who had followed them all day, Jesus asked God to provide enough food from a boy's lunch to feed the 5,000 *(Mark 6:32-44).*

Jesus modeled a life of prayer for His followers. *Luke 6:12* tells us that He prayed all night before choosing the twelve. We have seen how Jesus equipped His followers when they asked Him to teach them to pray *(Luke 11:1-4).*

Jesus also modeled servant leadership for His disciples when He washed their feet *(John 13:3-5).*

Fill in these blanks.

Jesus mentored His disciples by _____ them and by _____ what He wanted them to do.

Paul On Mentoring

Paul also was a mentor. The apostle trained leaders in every church he started. This is one reason he was able to establish as many churches as he did.

You have already seen that mentoring means modeling actions you want others to follow. Paul urged those in the Corinthian church to do just that.

Read *1 Corinthians 4:16.* What did Paul insist the Corinthians do?

Paul wrote, "I urge you to imitate me." The apostle wanted those who trusted his witness of Christ as Savior also to trust him in how they should live their life. We get our English word *mimic* from the Greek word translated *imitate.* Paul could say as a mentor, "mimic what I do."

Read *1 Corinthians 4:17.* Paul said Timothy would *"remind you of my way of life in Christ Jesus" (1 Cor. 4:17).* When Paul could not personally model for himself how he wanted the people to live, he sent an equipped follower. Timothy was someone he had mentored in the faith.

Paul was Timothy's mentor. The mature missionary taught Timothy to be a follower of Christ. Paul also taught him to be a servant leader.

Read *1 Timothy 4:12.* What did Paul tell Timothy to do for the believers in the church?

Paul told Timothy to be an example for the believers in the church. We get our English word *type* from the Greek word translated *example* in this verse. Paul wanted the members in the church to see in Timothy the type of disciple they should be.

In what areas of his life did Paul ask Timothy to demonstrate Christ?

Timothy was to model for the church what a life in Christ looked like in the areas of speech, daily living, love, faith, and purity. He was to mentor others by modeling the behavior he wanted in their lives. How did Timothy know what these things looked like? Paul mentored him. Mentoring means taking what you have caught from your mentor and sharing it with another.

Servant leaders in team ministry model how they want team members to act. Servant leaders model for others what Christ modeled for them.

Servant leaders model for others what Christ modeled for them.

In Need Of A Mentor

Explaining the "second promise of a Promise Keeper," Dr. Howard Hendricks writes:

"Every man reading this book should seek to have
three individuals in his life:
You need a Paul.
You need a Barnabas.
And you need a Timothy."[1]

While Promise Keepers is a ministry to men by men, this principle applies to everyone in the body of Christ, including students. (See *Titus 2:3-5.*) Dr. Hendricks encourages each believer to have a Paul in his life because "you need someone who's been down the road." Every believer needs a Barnabas because you need someone "who loves you but is not impressed by you." You also need a Timothy "into whose life you are building."[2] Servant leaders in team ministry need a pastor, a partner, and a protégé–someone whom they can train in servanthood. These people do not necessarily need to be on your ministry team, but they should be part of your ministry.

As a servant leader, you can be a mentor, and you need a mentor. Paul's words to Timothy teach you that even as a teenager you can be an example to others. You can be a mentor to those you lead. You also need a mentor to show you how to lead. Mentoring is part of servant leadership because it is how you prepare the next generation of leaders for service. Unless there are future leaders, there is no future.

Write the name of your mentor (or potential mentor) in the margin. Also write the name of someone you are mentoring or could mentor. This person may be a younger teenager just entering the youth group or who is a new Christian.

Personal Evaluation

1. Fill in the blanks with the words that teach T.E.A.M. ministry.

T _____

E _____

A _____

M _____

2. After this week of study and as you consider your ministry team, list some areas of need you might address as you begin to put your team together.

Summary

- Servant leaders are mentors to persons with them in team ministry. Mentoring is how the work of Christ passes on to the next generation of servant leaders. To mentor is to multiply Christ in the life of another.
- Jesus mentored His disciples by teaching them and by demonstrating the power of God in their lives.
- Paul was Timothy's mentor.
- Mentoring means taking what you have caught from your mentor and sharing it with another. Servant leaders model for others what Christ modeled for them.
- Servant leaders in team ministry need a mentor, a partner, and a protégé–someone whom they can train in servanthood.
- You are a mentor and need a mentor in your ministry as a servant leader.

[1]Excerpt from *Seven Promises of a Promise Keeper* by Howard G. Hendricks. Copyright © 1999, Promise Keepers. All rights reserved. International copyright secured. Used by permission.

[2]Ibid., 53-54.

Again, here is this week's memory verse, this time with a few more of the words omitted. Try completing the verse without looking back.

"Calling the Twelve to him, he _____ them out _____ _____ _____ and gave them _____ over evil spirits" (_____).

Take a few moments now to write a few statements here concerning what God has said to you this week through this verse, and how His words have become more meaningful in your life.

day 5

THE NEXT STEPS FOR A
SERVANT LEADER

Today You Will:

- Complete the study of *Jesus on Leadership*.
- Learn four next steps to becoming a servant leader.
- Make decisions about what you will do to continue the process of becoming a servant leader.
- Spend time in prayer concerning servant leadership and team ministry.

You have completed this important study of servant leadership. Hopefully, you have been inspired as you studied Jesus' teachings and examples of servant leadership. You have been encouraged by seeing how God has prepared you uniquely to serve Him. You have been challenged to equip someone for ministry and to team with others to reach a shared ministry goal. Now you may be asking, "What do I do next?" Or, "What do I do with all this information?"

Let's spend today completing a plan to help you continue this journey of servant leadership. It will involve four steps:

Step 1: Make Jesus' model of servant leadership the pattern for how you lead.

Step 2: Stay aware of how God is working in your life to mold you into a servant leader.

Step 3: Continue to seek ways to equip others for ministry.

Step 4: Team with others in ministry.

Step 1: *Make Jesus' model of servant leadership the pattern for how you lead.*

Look back at your journey through this study. You first experienced Jesus' teachings and examples of servant leadership (Week 1). These events and messages provided a completely new model of leadership for Jesus' disciples. *This model is the defining picture of how you should lead as a follower of Christ.* To follow Jesus is to lead like Jesus.

So, the first answer to your question, "What do I do next?" is to make Jesus' teachings and examples of servant leadership the benchmark for how you lead others. This will require a process of transforming your thinking and behavior *(Rom. 12:2)*. You will not lead this way naturally. You must allow Jesus to be your Master Teacher on leadership. You must take steps to spend time with the Master so He can empower you to lead as a servant leader.

> *Make Jesus' teachings and examples of servant leadership the benchmark for how you lead others.*

Here are some suggestions to continue this process. Place a check by the activity or activities you will do to continue learning to lead like Jesus.

- ☐ If I have not already done so, I will memorize *Mark 10:45* and apply it to my daily decisions.
- ☐ I will memorize the seven principles of servant leadership or carry them with me each day.
- ☐ I will study and seek to lead by these four major passages of Scripture that describe how Jesus led as a servant:
  - *Mark 10:35-45*
  - *John 13:3-11*
  - *Luke 14:7-11*
  - *Philippians 2:5-11*
- ☐ I will invite a friend to learn and apply these principles with me.
- ☐ I will ask someone who is a servant leader (youth minister or another church leader) to continue to mentor me in this process. Suggestions for further study can be found following today's work.

Step 2: *Stay aware of how God is working in your life to mold you into a servant leader.*

During Weeks 2 and 3, you considered how God gifted you spiritually, used experiences to shape your witness, molded the way you relate to others, is allowing you to gain vocational skills, and enthused you with His Spirit for ministry. This resulted in your S.E.R.V.E. profile (see p. 84). These become the tools of servant leadership that God is using to build the church. The church is the body of Christ, and you are an important member of that body. You are essential to how your local body of believers functions. All the other members also are essential. You alone do not have all the skills and gifts to carry out the mission of the church. The church works best when it works like a body rather than an institution.

Each part of who you are must be subjected to Jesus' example. Otherwise, you have merely finished another exercise in self-discovery. Stay aware of how God has worked and is continuing to work in your life, and allow the Holy Spirit to mold you into Jesus' model of servant leadership.

Ask yourself the following questions on a regular basis to be certain that you are on the right track as you join God where He is working in your church and community:

- How can I use God's spiritual gifts in my life to serve Him and His church? Where can I use these gifts most effectively?

- How do my life experiences affect how I see God, others, and myself? What is God doing in my life now to mold me into Christ's likeness?

> *God is working in your life to mold you into a servant leader.*

- How do my natural relational tendencies guide my behavior as a leader? In what ways must the Holy Spirit balance these tendencies to make me a stronger servant leader?

- How can I continually use my vocational skills as a servant leader? Am I learning new skills that I can implement in ministry?

- Who can I equip to find a place of servant leadership in the church?

- Who do I need on my ministry team who has a complementary S.E.R.V.E. profile?

STEP 3: *Continue to seek ways to equip others for ministry.*

Servant leaders equip others for ministry. Sometimes this is by actively teaching and leading them. At other times, it is simply by modeling a positive example of servant leadership. Leadership involves training those you lead so that they may be able to serve effectively.

Below is a checklist of actions which can help you as you seek to equip others.

❏ Keep a prayer list of people you sense are ready to serve in ministry. Pray daily for persons God would have you equip for service. Ask, Is this the person(s) You need me to invest in and equip for ministry?

❏ Regularly encourage those you are training. Write a note or send a small gift (ex: a coupon to a local ice cream shop) to let them know they are on the right track.

❏ One action you can take which will help you achieve success in team ministry is to know a person's S.E.R.V.E. profile before you ask him or her to serve in a particular ministry. Ask yourself, Does this person's gifts and abilities match the ministry I am asking him or her to do?

❏ Take time to listen to those you are equipping. Join them for lunch or invite them out for a snack. You also will want to observe them while they serve to understand how you can help them.

❏ Encourage those you lead to continue to grow in Christlikeness. What skills and attitudes must they learn to be effective in the ministry you have asked them to do?

❏ Pray often for those you are training. Without your prayers, they are helpless to succeed in ministry.

❏ Consider the resources at the end of this workbook as part of your continuing equipping process. (See page 126)

STEP 4: *Team with others in ministry.*

This week you learned that leadership is a team sport. You learned that team ministry is the most effective means for servant leaders. Use these suggestions to begin building your ministry team:

> *Servant leaders equip others for ministry.*

- Remember that T.E.A.M. ministry is not a complicated process. It can involve a group of teenagers who plan a Disciple Now weekend or reach out to students on their campus at school. Once your team has agreed on its goals, lead them to training opportunities that will enhance their gifts and abilities. Your pastor or minister of youth can help you in this important process.

- Plan fellowship events to build a sense of togetherness on your team. Spend time as a group in prayer about the needs God would have you team together to meet. With a Christlike spirit, be prepared to address any sense that the team is not together in direction or attitude. Be prepared to listen to their concerns and address their needs as important members of the team.

- Make sure you have empowered your team with the authority and resources to reach the shared goals of the group. Team members must feel that they have the necessary skills and opportunity to do their tasks.

- Create an ongoing sense of accountability among the team members. Be open to share how you have failed and how you need their help to reach the goals. Build a sense that each of you is accountable to God for the results of your ministry team.

> Remember that T.E.A.M. ministry is not a complicated process.

Personal Evaluation

The process of becoming a servant leader is never over. You have only begun this exciting journey. As you complete today's session, spend a special time in prayer. Consider the two statements below. Be prepared to share your commitments with your group.

- I will commit to continuing the process of becoming a servant leader by following the four suggested steps in this session.   ❏ Yes ❏ No

- As part of my role as a servant leader, I will encourage others to participate in a study of this resource. I will begin today praying for those persons God wants to encounter Jesus on leadership.   ❏ Yes ❏ No

Summary

The four suggested next steps in becoming a servant leader are:
1. Make Jesus' model of servant leadership the pattern for how you lead.
2. Stay aware of how God is working in your life to mold you into a servant leader.
3. Continue to seek ways to equip others for ministry.
4. Team with others in ministry.

Your commitment to live out the principles in this study will affect how you serve as a leader in your church or ministry.

You have completed this study of *Jesus on Leadership*. What one or two significant truths have you learned from this study? Record them here, and be prepared to share them with the group at your next meeting.

Mark 6:7
You've thought about this verse all week. Now try writing it completely from memory. For many people, memorizing Scripture is not easy. Do your best; check what you have written; and continue to be thankful for the blessing of God's Word now hidden in your heart forever.

YOUR NEXT STEPS TOWARD SERVANT LEADERSHIP

Once a child's first steps are taken, there is joy in the family. Yet with those first steps comes greater dependence on another for guidance, strength, direction, and assurance.

Your next steps toward maturing in Christian leadership can make all the difference in you, your church, and your community. As I have stated, this study is not the end of your understanding of servant leadership. A plan for continuing on and growing in this exciting time in your life could involve a study of other resources, including . . .

- *Experiencing God: Knowing and Doing the Will of God, Youth Edition* (0-8054-9925-3) by Henry Blackaby–This resource helps Christians experience God doing through them what only God can do.
- *Life in the Spirit, Youth Edition* (0-7673-2594-X) by Robertson McQuilkin–This biblical study of the Holy Spirit's power and activities helps Christians experience a deep and loving relationship with God, effectiveness in personal living, and ministry that makes a difference in our world.

- *The Mind of Christ, Youth Edition* (0-7673-0000-9) by T. W. Hunt–This course provides help for learning to think the thoughts of Christ. It is based on *Philippians 2:5-11: "Let this mind be in you, which was also in Christ Jesus."*
- *MasterLife: A Biblical Process for Growing Disciples, Student Edition* (0-7673-3495-7) by Avery T. Willis, Jr.–This classic study is in a format of two six-week courses in one workbook. As believers learn to practice six biblical disciplines, Jesus transforms their behavior; leads them to develop kingdom values; and involves them in His mission in the home, the church, and the world.
- *Share Jesus Without Fear: Students Reaching Students* (0-7673-3059-5) by William Fay and David Bennett–This evangelistic resource is an approach for sharing Jesus depending upon the power of the Holy Spirit and the Bible with no Scripture memory required. It helps participants overcome the fears of failure and rejection by obeying Christ.

Each of these resources is available by writing or calling the Customer Service Center, 1-800-458-2772; 127 Ninth Avenue North, Nashville, TN 37234-0113. They also are available by visiting the nearest LifeWay Christian Store serving you.

JESUS ON LEADERSHIP

Servant Leaders

S.E.R.V.E. God and
E.Q.U.I.P. Others for
T.E.A.M. Ministry

God Prepares Servant Leaders to S.E.R.V.E.

S piritual Gifts
E xperiences
R elational Style
V ocational Skills
E nthusiasm

Servant Leaders E.Q.U.I.P. Others

E ncourage Them to Serve
Q ualify Them for Service
U nderstand Their Needs
I nstruct Them
P ray for Them

Servant Leaders Serve in T.E.A.M. Ministry

T ogetherness
E mpowerment
A ccountability
M entoring

CHRISTIAN GROWTH STUDY PLAN: PREPARING CHRISTIANS TO GROW

In the **Christian Growth Study Plan,** this book, *Jesus on Leadership: Becoming a Servant Leader, Student Edition,* is a resource for course credit in three Leadership and Skill Development diploma plans. It is also a resource in the Christian Growth category subject area Ministry.

To receive credit in a group study that is 2.5 hours or more, attend the sessions and read the book. To receive credit for individual study, read the book, summarize the chapters, show your work to your pastor, a staff member, or other church leader.

Send this completed page to the Christian Growth Study Plan, 127 Ninth Avenue North, Nashville, TN 37234-0117; or FAX: (615) 251-5067. This page may be duplicated.

For information about the Christian Growth Study Plan, refer to the current *Christian Growth Study Plan Catalog.* Your church office may have a copy. If not, request a free copy from the Christian Growth Study Plan Office (615/251-2525).

Jesus on Leadership: Becoming a Servant Leader, Student Edition
COURSE NUMBER: CG-0514
COURSE/DIPLOMA CREDIT INFORMATION

Please check the appropriate box indicating the position you serve in your church. You may check more than one. You will receive course credit toward the diploma designed for your position(s).

❏ Leadership Development: for all church leaders (LS-0001)

❏ Church Leadership: for Discipleship Training directors, pastors, church staff, and other DT leaders (LS-0047)

❏ Associational Leadership: for Discipleship Training directors and other associational DT leaders (LS-0068)

❏ Christian Growth: Ministry (CG-0127)

PARTICIPANT INFORMATION

Social Security Number	Personal CGSP Number	Date of Birth
Name (First, MI, Last) ☐ Mr. ☐ Miss ☐ Mrs. ☐		Home Phone
Address (Street, Route, or P.O. Box)	City, State	Zip Code

CHURCH INFORMATION

Church Name		
Address (Street, Route, or P.O. Box)	City, State	Zip Code

CHANGE REQUEST ONLY

☐ Former Name		
☐ Former Address	(City, State)	Zip Code
☐ Former Church		Zip Code
Signature of Pastor, Conference Leader, or Other Church Leader		Date

*New participants are requested but not required to give SS# and date of birth. Existing participants, please give CGSP# when using SS# for the first time. Thereafter, only one ID# is required.